Craft Your Year

Craft Your Year
with
Sara Davies

THE CRAFTING BIBLE

SARA DAVIES

bantam

TRANSWORLD PUBLISHERS

Penguin Random House, One Embassy Gardens, 8 Viaduct Gardens, London SW11 7BW

www.penguin.co.uk

Transworld is part of the Penguin Random House group of companies
whose addresses can be found at global.penguinrandomhouse.com

First published in Great Britain in 2023 by Bantam
an imprint of Transworld Publishers

A CIP catalogue record for this book
is available from the British Library.

ISBN 9780857505149

Typeset in Mark Pro Light
Designed by Bobby Birchall, Bobby&Co.
Printed and bound in China by C&C Offset Printing Co., Ltd.

The authorized representative in the EEA is Penguin Random House Ireland,
Morrison Chambers, 32 Nassau Street, Dublin D02 YH68.

Penguin Random House is committed to a sustainable
future for our business, our readers and our planet.
This book is made from Forest Stewardship Council® certified paper.

For crafters and creators everywhere

Contents

Introduction   8

Spring   16

Summer   64

Autumn   106

Winter   142

Acknowledgements   190

Index   192

Introduction

For as long as I can remember, I've loved making things. I was introduced to crafting by the creative people in my life – my mam did flower arranging, my nana sewed, and my gran knitted and crocheted. When we were growing up, my sister Helen and I experimented with lots of popular crafting activities, such as salt dough, so you could say that crafting is definitely in our genes!

After creating my first ever product – a special tool to make bespoke envelopes for handmade cards, which was also the first of its kind – I was able to turn my love for crafting into a career. And I haven't looked back. I've been teaching and showing people how to create beautiful things for years now, and I thought it was high time that I shared my tips, tricks and ideas with you in this book to help you discover the joy of crafting too. So, whether you're a newbie or you're already hooked but looking for a new challenge, there's something for everyone.

For lots of people, crafting isn't just a fun hobby, it also has a really positive impact on their mental health and well-being because it gives them a creative outlet and reduces their stress levels. Plus, a great sense of achievement comes from making and finishing something yourself, so not only can crafting help to make you feel more calm, it can also improve your self-esteem.

With everyday life being so hectic and stressful, it can be tough to find 'you time'. Trying to take some quality time to unwind after a busy day at work or a manic school run can be difficult. That being said, even if you can carve out ten minutes to get creative, or have the luxury of an hour, I promise you that time will always be worth it. Putting your hands to work helps to immerse you in the moment and gives you a much-needed break from the pressures of everyday life.

You don't have to spend lots of money buying expensive equipment either – I'm all for making use of what you already have lying around your home. I'm a huge fan of upcycling things too, rather than splurging or picking up one-use items, so that's exactly what you'll find in these pages.

When I started my crafting journey, I quickly discovered that crafters want to improve, develop their skills and learn new things, and the same goes for me! That's why every craft in this book includes easy-to-follow how-to steps with images to guide you through the creative process, along with handy hints and top tips.

From the calming effect of the repetitive knotting of macramé to creating stunning seasonal wreaths and creative cards for special occasions throughout the year, I hope you find inspiration and a lot of new knowledge within these pages. Whether you're looking for an idea for a Christmas decoration or a home-décor piece for the spring, I've got you covered. With crafts for every season and every ability, you'll find projects to bring you and your family creative fun and joy while improving your skills along the way.

So, what are you waiting for? Turn the page and let's get crafting!

Conversion Table

In my experience, the world of crafting continues to use imperial units of measurement, so I've used them in this book. If you prefer to work in metric, most tape measures and weighing scales display both units, or you can use Google for quick conversions. I've included a few rounded conversions below in case helpful.

Inches	Centimetres
2	5
4	10
6	15
12	30

Ounces	Grams
2	57
4	113
8	227

Fluid ounces	Litres
34	1

Toolkit

As you turn the pages of this book, try new projects and find new confidence in your craft and creativity, certain tools and supplies will become familiar faces! These are my tried-and-true craft essentials; tools that I always have at my fingertips. Here's what you need to know . . .

1 Medium scissors (these are essential!)

2 Strong PVA glue

3 Glue tape pen

4 Large scissors for larger areas

5 Glue gun (I would definitely recommend buying one of these if you don't already own one. They're fairly inexpensive and something you'll use time and time again!)

6 Textile glue for fabrics

7 Scoring tool

8 Small scissors (for precision snipping and fiddly bits)

9 Double-sided tape

10 Pokey tool (for creating fine holes and tackling extremely delicate projects)

11 Red liner tape

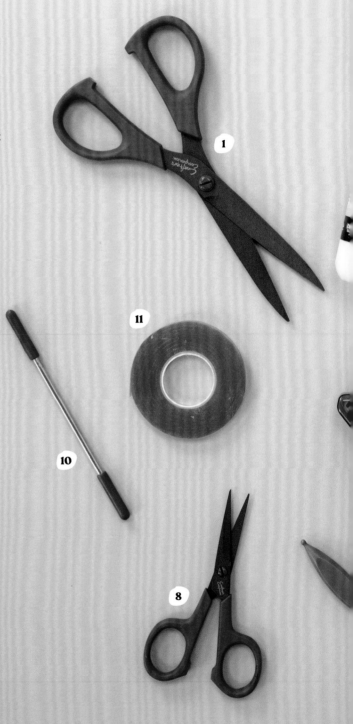

Glossary

If you're new to crafting, or perhaps a seasoned maker interested in a refresher, here are some key words and phrases that you'll often see.

Acetate
A clear, see-through film perfect for making pretty windows on cards, boxes and other papercrafting projects.

Adhesive
A substance that sticks one item to another. It can come in various forms, such as spray, wet glue, tape and so on.

Card stock
Material used in cardmaking, available in a number of weights, colours and textures.

Cutting mat
A cutting surface that will protect your work area. Can be made from a soft, self-healing material, or from toughened, tempered glass, which is also a great choice to use with some inking techniques.

Die-cutting
A technique where metal dies are used in a manual or electronic machine to cut words, shapes and designs into a range of materials, including card, fabric, foil and more.

Distress
A technique to give an aged or vintage look to a material.

Embellishment
An additional decorative detail or feature to make a project more appealing.

Fabric stabilizer
Often available as a spray, this liquid formula allows you to shape fabric or trims which will stiffen upon drying.

Fussy cutting
To deliberately cut a section of fabric or paper to showcase a particular pattern or print.

Guillotine
A tool used for cutting card and paper. A bladed arm is lifted, the card/paper is moved into position and the arm is brought down to cut the card.

Markers
Pens with a self-contained ink source, and a nib made from a porous fibre.

Mat and layer
A technique used in papercrafting to create layers of borders, usually in different colours, which results in a topper or sentiment standing out from the background.

Skein
A length of thread or yarn, loosely coiled and knotted.

Spring

Organizer

For me, January is all about fresh starts and opportunities, and there's no better way to channel that energy into a craft project than by creating this super handy organizer.

You can use it to arrange notes on appointments, the kids' after-school activities, shopping lists, photos, meal plans, loose pens, your car keys . . . You name it, you can pop it on the organizer to remind you.

You will need:

- Glue gun
- Glue sticks
- Frame with removable backing
- Cork fabric
- Felt or fabric of your choosing
- Large scissors
- Ribbon
- Fabric glue

TOP TIP Swap out the darker tones used in the project for a colour that complements your own style!

1 Plug in the glue gun to heat up.

2 Remove the glass or Perspex from the frame then measure a strip of cork fabric to cover roughly the top third of the frame's backing board.

3 Once the cork has been trimmed to size, use the glue gun to adhere it to the top third of the backing board **(step A)**.

4 Next, create some pockets. Trim some felt or fabric and glue it in place to cover the bottom two thirds of the frame backing **(step B)**.

5 Take another, shorter piece of fabric of the same width and place it slightly further down the backing. You only need to add the adhesive to the bottom edge and sides.

6 Repeat this process to create another smaller pocket.

7 Next, cut three lengths of ribbon to line the top of each pocket and the strip where the felt fabric meets the cork. Use fabric glue for this step, if you have some, otherwise a small amount of glue from the glue gun will be fine **(steps C and D)**.

8 Put the backing board back into the frame and you're ready to get organized in style!

Rose and Aloe Vera Clay Face Mask

I started making this face mask back in my *Strictly* days when I was on the show and doing the tour. It was such a treat to have my face made up to the nines every day, but it did take a bit of a toll on my skin. So, to rehydrate and give my skin some much needed TLC, I started treating myself to a face mask once a week!

However, I have always been a bit sceptical about the chemicals that are found in off-the-shelf masks. I did a bit of research and I've been making my own formulation since then, which is great because I know exactly what's in it and it's a luxury treat for the skin that I can whip up in a few minutes!

You will need:

- ½ tablespoon aloe vera gel (moisturizing and soothing)
- ½ tablespoon rose water (reduces redness and contains antioxidants)
- 1 tablespoon pink clay powder (can contribute to brighter skin and removes excess oils)
- Small non-metallic bowl
- Face cloth (optional)

TOP TIP This face mask is best made fresh but you can store it in a fridge to give the mask a cool and refreshing feel.

1 Add the face-mask ingredients to the bowl and mix well to a thick but spreadable consistency that is terracotta-like in colour **(steps A and B)**.

2 Using your fingers or a face-mask spatula, apply the mask to your face. Take care not to get any too close to your eyes.

3 Leave the mask on your skin for around 15–20 minutes then remove with a damp face cloth or by rinsing your face with some warm water.

4 And *voilà* – amazing-feeling skin in under 30 minutes! If you have any of the mask left, store it in a small pot in the fridge and use within a week.

TAKE CARE! Always do a
patch test on sensitive skin.

Foot Scrub

Here is another of my routines that I picked up while filming *Strictly*, because my feet were constantly in bits, which probably won't come as a shock to anyone! They desperately needed some extra TLC. I continued to make this DIY foot scrub because it smells incredible, is super easy to create and leaves your feet feeling silky smooth.

If you need a bit of a pick-me-up or you're in the mood for a self-care evening, then this is the project for you. The best part is, you probably have most of these ingredients in your kitchen cupboards!

This recipe will make enough for two small jars – I was batch-making this for my *Strictly* friends! So if you do want a smaller amount, simply halve the ingredients set out below.

You will need:

- 250g caster sugar (exfoliating)
- 120g coconut oil (moisturizing properties)
- 1 tablespoon spirulina powder (contains lots of antioxidants and vitamins)
- 1 peppermint tea bag
- 10–12 drops of peppermint essential oil
- Glass bowl
- One large, or two small, clean, lidded, airtight glass jars for storage

1 Collect your ingredients: the sugar, coconut oil, spirulina powder, tea bag contents and peppermint oil **(step A)**.

2 Mix together in a bowl.

3 Transfer the mixture to one large or two small, lidded jars, or take it to the bathroom and use it straight away **(step B).** It really is that easy!

4 Store the remainder of the foot scrub in the fridge and use within six weeks.

Spring Wreath

A wreath is a fantastic way to make a statement before visitors even have a chance to step through your door! Wreath-making is something I started doing with my mam and my sister Helen a few Christmases ago, using a wire frame and some fresh foliage, and it's a tradition that we've kept up every year since.

This spring version made with faux flowers is so easy to piece together, even if you've not made a wreath before. The finished result is something you can bring out every single year!

You will need:

- Glue gun
- Glue sticks
- Natural willow wreath
- Assortment of pampas grass
- Assortment of artificial flowers
- Twine
- Hessian ribbon
- Scissors

1   Plug in your glue gun to heat up.

2   Once you've decided on the placement of your pampas grass, start adding it to the wreath. Do this first so that it sits in the background as the base layer. Set it on an angle on both sides and fan out some of the pieces before securing it in place using the glue gun **(step A)**.

3   Next, begin to arrange the faux flowers and glue them in place. Tuck some of the blooms just inside the wreath and around the front of it to create dimension **(step B)**.

4   If you need to create a hanging for the wreath, tie a length of twine around the top of the willow hoop and secure it in place with a knot. Cut an additional length of twine and tie it around the first to create a loop. To finish things off, create a bow from some hessian ribbon and glue into position.

Pompom Making

Who remembers when the best way to make a pompom was to cut out a circle from an old cardboard cereal box? I do! I also remember how it used to take absolutely ages and your arm would ache from winding the wool around the template.

Well, I'm here to change your life because pompom makers are the bomb.com! Once you have one of these amazingly useful kits, which contain a number of pompom makers to create different sizes of pompom, you will never go back! A bold statement, I know, but trust me – you will love them!

You will need:

- Pompom-maker kit
- Ball of wool
- Scissors

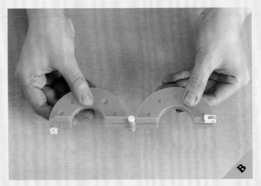

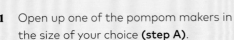

1   Open up one of the pompom makers in the size of your choice **(step A)**.

2   Match the two halves of the maker so that the bumps fit inside the grooves of the tool **(step B)**.

3   Begin to wrap the yarn around one half of the maker tool **(step C)**.

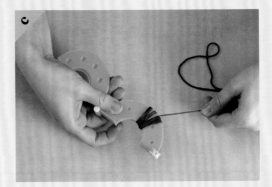

4 Keep wrapping until the first half of the tool is completely covered with yarn and there are no visible gaps.

5 Repeat the process for the other half of the maker **(step D)**.

6 Snip the wool free from the ball **(step E)**.

7 Close the two halves of the pompom maker together and secure using the latches **(step F)**.

8 Snip the threads of yarn around the outside of the circle. Your scissors will fit between the two halves of the pompom maker and allow you to follow the circle **(step G)**.

9 A pompom shape should now be starting to form on either side of the tool **(step H)**.

10 Once all the threads have been cut, take a length of yarn, slot it into the gap between the two halves of the maker tool and tie it securely around the pompom shape **(steps I and J)**.

11 Remove the two halves of the maker **(step K)**.

12 Trim the pompom to neaten its shape if necessary. And there you have it – a fabulous pompom! How easy was that?

Gift Bag

Let's talk gift bags! Nice gift bags can be really expensive to buy but paper is fairly inexpensive, so why not make your own? I love this project because it's super quick and quite easy. Once you have this technique under your belt you can experiment with a variety of different-sized pieces of paper to create an endless supply of gift bags for every season.

You will need:

- 12" x 12" piece of patterned paper
- Glue tape pen
- Hole punch
- Length of ribbon or twine

1   Take your 12" x 12" piece of patterned paper **(step A)**.

2   Fold the left-hand side in a little over halfway.

3   Fold the right-hand side over the left, so that it overlaps slightly **(step B)**, and glue into place **(steps C and D)**.

TOP TIP   Practise on a scrap piece of paper so that you don't risk wasting a nice piece on your first attempt!

4   Fold the bottom of the bag up approximately 3 inches and make sure that it is well creased **(step E)**.

5   Open the bottom part of the flap you've just created and fold the two sides in towards the centre – you should be left with a diamond-like shape **(step F)**.

6   Fold the bottom part of the flap up to the centre of the diamond shape **(step G)**.

7   Fold the top part of the flap downwards, on top of the last fold, so that the two pieces are overlapping slightly. Glue into place **(step H)**.

8   Fold both sides of the bag in towards the join you've just made **(step I)**.

9   Unfold the bag and push both sides inwards **(step J)**.

10 Refold the bag and punch two holes at its opening. Thread a length of ribbon or twine through the holes and tie into a bow to close the bag **(step K)**.

Valentine's Day Gift Box

Whether you celebrate the official day of love or not, this gift-box project is a great one to learn because it can be customized for special occasions throughout the year. I find that gift boxes and bags can be a bit pricey, but this gorgeous box can be made from any paper and card you have to hand.

You can fit all sorts inside – sweets or chocolates, jewellery, soaps, hair accessories . . . you name it!

TOP TIP There are quite a few steps to this project, but once you get to grips with the technique, it will become second nature. Practise on a piece of scrap card first!

You will need:

- 6" x 12" red card, plus extra for rolled flowers
- Scoring tool or pencil
- Ruler
- Black card
- Pink patterned paper
- Scissors or paper guillotine
- Glue gun
- Glue sticks
- Glue tape pen
- Hole punch
- Pokey tool
- 2 lengths of ribbon (roughly 18" each) in different widths
- White gel pen

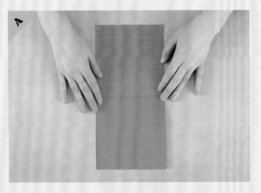

To create the box:

1   Fold your 6" x 12" piece of red card in half to create two 6" x 6" squares **(step A)**.

2   Locate the midway point of each of the short edges of the card. Using a ruler, either score or draw a line between those points and the outer edges of the centre fold of the card **(step B)**.

3 With each line, keep the ruler in place and fold the outer edge of the card over the top. Run the edge of your pencil or scoring tool along each fold to reinforce it **(step C)**.

4 You should now have four triangle-shaped flaps **(step D)**.

5 Place your hands around each of the sides and bring them together so that they close to form a triangular box **(step E)**.

To decorate the box:

1 Plug in your glue gun to heat up.

2 To decorate the front of the box, cut a triangle from some black card – each side should measure 5½ inches. Create another triangle slightly smaller than this from your pink patterned paper. This is to go on top of the black card. It should have a narrow black border when in place – this technique is called a mat and layer. Glue the patterned triangle to the black triangle using the tape pen **(step F)**.

3 Create two more triangular mat and layers for the other sides of the box.

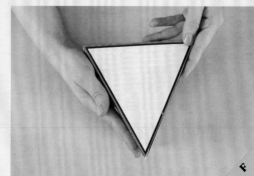

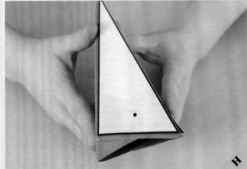

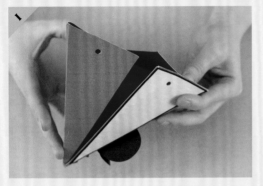

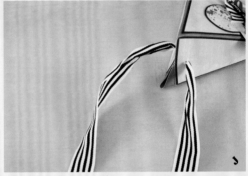

4 Use the tape pen to glue the triangles to the front and the sides of the box **(step G)**.

5 Close each side of the box and use a hole punch, pokey tool or pencil to create some holes in each of the closing sides **(steps H and I)**.

6 Thread a length of ribbon through the holes to secure the box **(step J)**.

7 Draw a heart shape on some black card and cut it out. Repeat to create a slightly smaller heart shape from your pink patterned paper. Mat and layer this onto the black heart.

8 Using the tape pen, glue the heart to the front left-hand side of the box.

9 Create two small roses from red card (using the rolled-flower technique from page 44) and 2–3 leaves from black card. Fashion some small bow shapes from different lengths and widths of ribbon.

10 Use the glue gun to fix the roses, leaves and ribbon in place over the heart.

11 Using a white gel pen, write 'Be mine' (or your message of choice) onto some black card and cut it out.

12 To finish, glue your message in place on the front of the card.

Valentine's Wooden Photo Cube

My favourite thing about making something myself is the personal touch I can bring to a project, and the knowledge that I created the whole thing from start to finish.

This wooden cube is a perfect example of one of those super personal projects. Not only is it a great way to display cherished memories but it also looks really trendy and chic.

You will need:

- Photocopier paper
- Printer
- Wooden cube
- Mod Podge
- Small paintbrush
- Clean cloth

1 Select four of your favourite images to print out. You will need to size each one to fit onto a cube face and print it as a mirror image so that it transfers correctly. To do this, flip the image in your photo editing software of choice, resize it and print out onto regular photocopier paper. Spread a layer of Mod Podge over the wooden surface of one of the cube's faces **(step A)**.

2 Lay your first image print-side down over the block, making sure its edges are lined up correctly. Press it down firmly onto the Mod Podge-covered surface.

3 Let it dry for about 30 minutes.

4 Wet your cloth under a tap until it's damp but not soaking.

5 Use the cloth to gently rub the paper away from the surface of the block. The paper will come away, leaving the image on the block, in a similar way to a temporary tattoo transfer **(step B)**.

6 Keep rubbing until all of the paper has come away from the image **(step C)**. You may even be able to peel some of the paper away with your fingers.

7 Repeat steps 2–6 for the remaining three images.

8 Leave to dry for around 30 minutes then spread a thin layer of Mod Podge over each face to seal the images in place.

9 If you want to create a Valentine's-inspired square for the top of your block, simply choose a piece of card with a suitable design, cut to size, glue in place using Mod Podge **(steps D and E)** and set aside to dry for 30 minutes.

10 Enjoy gifting your wooden cube to someone special!

Mother's Day Card

Learning a new card-making technique is so fulfilling because it allows you to go on and create handmade cards time and time again. I always find that people love to receive handmade cards because they really appreciate the thought and effort that goes into them. This project is simple but effective.

1 Create a white 5" x 7" card base, or use a ready-made one if you have one already **(step A)**.

2 Stick your first 2" x 2" paper square onto your card base. Position it slightly off centre and rotated 90 degrees into a diamond shape **(step B)**.

3 You really have free rein with the placement and pattern of your squares as the design will all come together. Just make sure that the edges of the squares are touching one another.

4 Carry on decorating the front of the card by gluing the squares in place in diagonal rows. Trim away any excess paper that may hang over the edges of the card **(steps C and D)**.

5 Once all of the squares have been glued in place, create a patchwork effect along the edges of each

You will need:

- White 5" x 7" card base (you can make this yourself by folding in half a piece of white card measuring 14" x 5", or pick up ready-made versions in most arts and crafts stores)
- 2" x 2" patterned paper squares (cut 12 in total so you have a few spares)
- Scissors or paper guillotine
- Glue tape pen
- Black fine liner pen
- Pencil and ruler
- Some white card (can be offcuts)
- Some black card (can be offcuts)
- Coloured gel pen of choice
- Small foam pads

square by using a fine liner pen to draw on some faux stitches **(step E)**.

6 Use a pencil and a ruler to draw a small rectangle or ribbon-edge shape onto a piece of black card. Repeat the design on a piece of white card but make it slightly smaller in size so that you can mat and layer it on top of the black card.

7 Use a pen to write 'Happy Mother's Day' onto the piece of white card.

8 Add some small foam pads to the back of the sentiment to give it some dimension, remove the film backing from the adhesive then position your message onto the front of your card to complete your design!

Bath Salts Jar

If you're celebrating someone special for Mother's Day, or if you're looking for a last-minute gift, why not have a go at making this bath salts jar? I can't even begin to tell you how easy it is and it looks absolutely gorgeous.

Plus, each layer of ingredients has different properties, all of which combine to deliver the most relaxing bath-time experience!

You will need:

- Clean airtight glass jar
- Epsom salts (help to ease aches and pains)
- Dried flower petals (look really pretty)
- Dried lavender (relaxing properties)
- Coconut milk powder (moisturizing properties)
- Small spoon, to transfer contents to jar

1 Collect your ingredients **(step A)**.

2 Using a spoon, begin to build up the layers of ingredients in the jar, starting with the Epsom salts **(step B)**.

3 The Epsom-salts layers should be the thickest, at around an inch, while the other layers can be half an inch each.

4 Keep alternating the products used in each layer until you have filled the entire jar **(step C)**.

Flower Heart Frame

How sweet is this flower heart frame? I'm always on the lookout for projects that will make great gifts, and this rose heart frame would make a lovely Mother's Day, Valentine's Day or birthday gift. I actually made this for my mam a couple of years ago and added a 'mam' vinyl onto the glass of the frame as a personal touch.

TOP TIP You can use this rolled-flower technique on lots of different projects, such as gift boxes, cards and loads more.

You will need:

- Glue gun
- Glue sticks
- Pencil
- Circle template (I used a standard mug)
- 5 A4 sheets of pink paper
- Scissors
- Pokey tool
- Shadow box frame
- PVA glue

1   Plug in your glue gun to heat up.

2   Use a pencil to draw around your chosen template on a piece of pink paper **(step A)**.

3   Use your scissors to cut out the circle **(step B)** then begin to cut a spiral shape into it. Make sure to maintain as equal a width as possible when creating the spiral **(step C)**.

4 Continue to cut the spiral shape until you reach the centre of your circle **(step D)**.

5 Hold the beginning of the spiral and use a pokey tool or a similarly pointed instrument to roll the paper spiral around it **(step E)**.

6 Once you have completely rolled the spiral shape around the tool, slide it off gently and open it out very slightly to form the flower shape **(step F)**.

7 Repeat steps 1–6 until you have twenty-five paper flowers in total.

8 Next, create a black card base, large enough to fit onto the back of the frame and fill the visible window area of the shadow box frame **(step G)**.

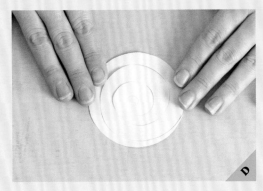

9 Take some white card and, using the glue gun or some PVA glue, mat and layer this square onto the black piece of card **(step H)**.

10 Use the rolled flowers to map out a heart shape in the centre of the white card. Check their placement carefully before securing them into place with the

glue gun. If you need a guide, sketch this out with a pencil first **(steps I, J and K)**.

11 Set aside to dry for 30 minutes. Once dry, place the finished piece back into the shadow box frame.

12 Gift your beautiful flower frame to a loved one or keep it for yourself!

Easter Treat Jars

These Easter jars are the perfect craft project. They're great to make with kids because they're really simple and fun, but the added bonus is that they look really cute dotted round the house at Easter. They add an instant pop of colour and, once filled with different types of edible eggs and Easter treats, they're guaranteed to be a hit with kids and adults alike. Craft and chocolate – what's not to love?!

1   In pencil, draw or trace a rabbit or egg shape onto some card.

2   Carefully cut out the shape with some scissors **(step A)**.

3   Take the temporary adhesive and spray the section of the jar where you'd like the shape to sit.

4   Use your fingers to press the shape into place. Ensure that it's completely flat and stuck to the jar's surface.

5   Paint the jar with your acrylic paint of choice, including around and over the top of the card shape **(step B)**.

You will need:

- Card or paper (this won't be part of the final jar, so feel free to use scrap paper)
- Pencil
- Scissors
- Clean jars with lids
- Temporary adhesive spray
- Acrylic paint (pastel shades work well for Easter)
- Paint brush
- Length of twine or ribbon
- Mini chocolate eggs or Easter-inspired treats

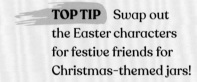

TOP TIP Swap out the Easter characters for festive friends for Christmas-themed jars!

6   Set the jar aside to dry for 30 minutes.

7   If you think it needs another coat of paint, apply and leave to dry for another 30 minutes.

8   Once the paint is dry, peel the shape away from the glass. As the shape has been temporarily stuck in place, it should leave behind a rabbit- or egg-shaped silhouette, which will act as a window into your treat jar.

9   Loop a length of twine or ribbon around the neck of your jar and tie into a bow.

10 Fill your jar with your Easter treats of choice, pop on the lid and you're good to go!

Easter Bunny Wreath

Easter and spring wreaths have increased in popularity in recent years and I've seen a few types of bunny wreaths out there. However, I absolutely love the style of this loop wreath. It's so satisfying to make, and you can personalize it to your own taste with your choice of artificial flowers. It's the perfect way to brighten up a front door in springtime!

You will need:

- Glue gun
- Glue sticks
- 2–3 skeins (3½oz) of white loop yarn (soft yarn with a looped effect)
- 12" natural grapevine wreath
- 9" natural grapevine wreath
- Faux flowers of your choice
- 2 lengths organza ribbon measuring 12"
- 4 lengths hessian ribbon measuring 24"
- 12 pipe cleaners
- Piece of card measuring 2" x 6"

1 Plug in your glue gun to heat up.

2 Wrap the loop yarn around the large and small wreaths, leaving enough yarn at the ends to tie the two wreaths together **(step A)**.

3 Using the glue gun, arrange and attach some faux flowers to the top of the larger wreath, along with a small bow fashioned from organza ribbon **(step B)**.

4 Tie the two wreaths together, making sure that they are secure.

5 Glue six pipe cleaners to one of the hessian strips – three at each end with a slight gap in the middle. This will ensure

that your bunny ears hold their shape when in place **(step C)**.

6 Using the glue gun, stick the second hessian ribbon strip on top of the first strip to conceal the pipe cleaners **(step D)**.

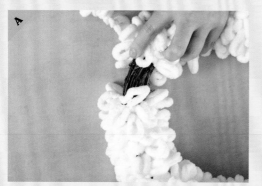

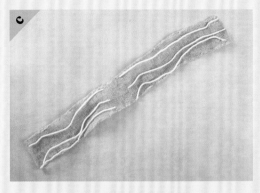

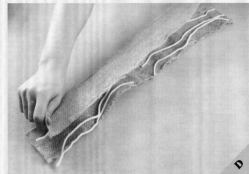

7 Bend the long strip in half and glue the two ends together to complete your first bunny ear **(step E)**.

8 Repeat steps 5–7 to create the second ear.

9 Glue both ears to the top of the smaller wreath. Then, glue your pre-cut strip of card over the ends of the ears, behind the bunny's head, to keep them securely in place **(step F)**.

10 Loop the remaining piece of organza ribbon around the top of the wreath, between the bunny ears, to create a hanging for your door, or simply lean against a mantelpiece.

Pompom Easter Bunny Pots

If you're hosting a party, a special Sunday lunch or an egg hunt this year then these little upside-down bunny pots are an absolute must. They make the cutest placeholders or decorations and, best of all, you can bargain with the kids to help you out with colouring in the bunny feet in exchange for some sweet treats.

You will need:

- Glue gun
- Glue sticks
- White pompoms (see page 26 for a refresher on pompom making)
- Green card
- Pencil
- Scissors
- Mini terracotta plant pots (or any small pots)
- Cotton wool balls
- White card
- Pink marker pen
- Mini blackboard posts and chalk

1   Plug in your glue gun to heat up.

2   Create a white pompom big enough to fit inside your pot with the top sticking out.

3   Draw five or six blades of grass onto your green card and cut out the pieces with some scissors **(step A)**.

4   Arrange the blades of grass inside the rim of your pot and fix into place using the glue gun **(step B)**.

5   Add a small amount of glue to the bottom sides of the pompom and push it into your pot – far enough for it to stick into place but with enough of the pompom poking out of the top **(step C)**.

6   Take a cotton wool ball and glue it to the middle of the pompom to look like a bunny's tail **(step D)**.

7   Next, draw two bunny feet onto a piece of white card. Cut these out.

8   Using a pink marker pen, draw and colour in the paw-pad area of the foot **(step E)**.

9   Fix these in place using the glue gun **(step F)**.

10 Write your chosen name on a mini blackboard using some chalk then tuck it into the pot beside the blades of grass. There you have it – a little upside-down bunny pot ready for the Easter season!

Macramé Plant Hanger

I love challenging myself and trying out new crafts, especially when I need five minutes to relax during a busy day! Last year, I started to experiment with the popular trend of macramé and have been working my way up to tackling some bigger projects. This plant hanger is fab and a relatively easy project to try if you're still a beginner or fancy practising your macramé techniques.

You will need:

- Ball of chunky jute twine or yarn
- Scissors
- Measuring tape
- Plant pot and plant

1   Begin by cutting nine lengths of jute twine or yarn. If you want to create a regular hanger for an average-size plant, each length should be approximately 6 feet, but you can adjust according to your preference.

2   Once you have your nine lengths of twine or yarn, fold them in half and secure the folded section a little further down with a small length of string. This provides you with a small loop from which to hang your macramé pot holder (**step A**).

3   When you hold your piece by the loop, you should have eighteen strings of 4 feet each.

4   Divide the eighteen strings into three sections made up of six strings each (**step B**).

5   Divide each bunch into three again, with two strands each, and create three separate braids about 14 inches long (**step C**).

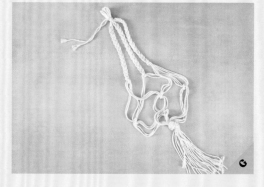

6 Tie a double knot in the end of each braid to secure it **(step D)**.

7 You should now have just over 6 inches from each braid knot hanging loose. Divide the strings into two, so you have two lots of three strings in each.

8 Next, gather one of the groups of three strings with an adjacent group of three strings and tie them together with a double knot **(step E)**.

9 Repeat until all three braids have been connected in this way **(step F)**.

10 Next, measure a further 6 inches along the strings and bring all eighteen strands together in a large knot **(step G)**.

11 Finally, trim the strings until you are satisfied with their length. Place your potted plant in the macramé holder, stand back and enjoy your handiwork!

Origami Flowers

It's widely known that crafting is really good for our well-being, and mindful crafting is a phrase that comes up time and time again. When I think of mindful crafting, this origami-flowers project is the first thing that springs to mind.

Crafting paper flowers is the perfect activity for switching off from our everyday lives and doing nothing other than getting creative with our hands. Perfecting each of the folds is unbelievably satisfying, and once you've made one of these flowers, you'll want to make more and more.

Trust me when I say everyone I have taught to do these has been hooked!

You will need:

- Glue gun
- Glue sticks
- 8" x 8" paper squares (5 squares per flower that you'd like to make)
- 12" wooden skewers
- Vase

1 Plug in the glue gun to heat up.

2 Take one of the paper squares and position it so that one of its corners is directly in front of you (**step A**).

3 Fold the square in half, corner to corner (**step B**).

TOP TIP This project is perfect for teens or for something different to try during a coffee-morning catch-up with friends.

4 Fold the right-hand side of the triangle inwards so that the bottom right corner meets the top point of the triangle **(step C)**.

5 Repeat step 4 for the left-hand side **(step D)**.

6 Place a finger inside one of the folds that you have made, open it out and

flatten it. It should create a kite shape with a crease down the centre **(steps E and F)**.

7 Tuck and crease the top section of the kite shape into the fold so that it's hidden out of sight **(step G)**.

8 Repeat steps 6–7 on the other side **(step H)**.

9 Fold the two outer triangles in half, using the existing centre crease of that section as a guide **(step I)**.

10 Cup the shape into your hand so that the two outer edges meet in the middle and the paper forms a whole petal shape **(step J)**.

11 Repeat steps 2–10 a further four times to create five petals in total **(step K)**.

12 Using the glue gun, stick the petals to one another and glue a wooden skewer in their centre. It's easier to do the second part of this step once two or three of the petals are glued together **(step L)**.

13 Set your flower aside to dry for at least 30 minutes.

14 Continue to create as many paper blooms as you like.

15 When your origami flowers have dried, display them together in your favourite vase!

No-sew Cushion Cover

One really easy way to give a room a bit of an update is to replace the soft furnishings, and it doesn't have to cost the earth! For instance, I'm such a fan of this simple no-sew cushion-cover hack. No needles, thread or sewing required – I promise.

These covers also make a great Mother's Day gift – all you need is a nice bit of fabric, a cushion pad, and *voilà*! You'll have instant bragging rights for how you made the lovely, personalized cushion cover sitting proudly somewhere in your mam's house.

You will need:

- Length of fabric of your choice
- Cushion pad
- Fabric scissors

1   Roll out your length of fabric and have your cushion pad to hand.

2   To make the cover, the fabric will need to be three times as wide as the cushion and twice as deep. Use the cushion itself to measure this out accordingly.

3   Cut the piece of fabric to size using your fabric scissors.

4   Position the cushion in the centre of the fabric and fold in the left-hand half of the material to the centre of the cushion **(step A)**.

5   Repeat with the right-hand half of the fabric and fold it across to the centre **(step B)**.

6 Fold each side of the fabric to create a triangle as you would when wrapping a gift, making sure the edges are nice and neat **(step C)**.

7 Bring both sides of the fabric to the centre and tie together with a knot **(step D)**.

8 Tuck away the ends of the fabric to finish the look **(step E)** and be very impressed with your brand-new cushion cover!

TOP TIP This handy technique isn't reserved exclusively for cushion covers. For an eco-friendly alternative to wrapping paper, why not follow the same steps to gift wrap a box?

Doily LED Candle Holder

For lots of people, when they think of fabric stabilizer (if they have heard of it at all!) the image that comes to mind immediately is a wet, starchy liquid used to add structure and stiffness to shirt collars. In fact, this super versatile liquid has many different uses, and I have found so much enjoyment in the different projects that you can use it for – one of my favourite Halloween projects on page 112, for example.

These doily LED candle holders are beautifully delicate-looking and will add a touch of modern class to any room. They're so simple to create and are guaranteed to start your love affair with fabric stabilizer!

You will need:

- Ramekin
- Cling film
- Tray or work surface that you don't mind getting a bit messy
- Fabric stabilizer
- Medium-sized bowl
- Fabric doily of your choice

1   Turn your ramekin upside down, then drape some cling film across its base so that it slightly overhangs. Set this to one side on your tray or work surface **(step A)**.

2   Next, unscrew the lid of the fabric stabilizer and pour a generous quantity of it into a bowl.

3   Take your doily and use your hands to completely submerge it in the fabric stabilizer. Make sure that the doily

film inside the ramekin and scrunch the outer edges of the doily to give it a curled edge **(steps B and C)**.

5   Set aside to dry overnight.

6   When the doily has dried and hardened, flip it over and remove the cling film-covered ramekin. This should be fairly easy to do as the cling film will have been scrunched inside **(step D)**.

is soaked through by leaving it in the stabilizer for a few minutes.

7   You're now ready to fill your doily holder with an LED candle or some trinkets!

4   Lift the doily out of the bowl and drape it over the bottom of the cling film-covered ramekin. Tuck any excess cling

Summer

Water Effect Flower Vase

I love having a mix of bits I've made and bought around the house, and I am chuffed with how well this water-effect vase turned out.

You can use any artificial flowers you like. Once the glue dries clear, it holds the stones and stems in place and the illusion is one of beautiful flowers in real water. Honestly, it's a super easy project to have a go at!

You will need:

- Glass vase
- Clear PVA glue
- Selection of stones and pebbles
- Faux flowers and stems (I used an artificial orchid)

1   Fill your vase almost halfway with clear PVA glue **(step A)**.

2   Start to add the stones and pebbles to the vase, one by one. The glue level will start to rise as you do so **(step B)**.

3   Keep adding the stones and pebbles until there is a gap of about an inch between them and the top of the vase, and add more glue, if necessary. There shouldn't be too much space between the pebbles, so ensure that everything is nicely packed in **(step C)**.

4   Start to arrange your artificial flowers and stems in the spaces between the pebbles, and position them in a way that you like **(step D)**.

5   That's it! Set aside on a flat surface to dry overnight.

TOP TIP The glue will take several hours to dry, so if you decide to tweak the placement of the flowers, you will have some time to do so.

Floral Macramé Wreath

This project combines beautiful artificial blooms with macramé techniques to create a stunning floral wreath hanging. The understated colours in this wreath make it an ideal decoration for a dressing room, bedroom or even a nursery space.

You will need:

- Glue gun
- Glue sticks
- Ball of macramé yarn
- Scissors
- Metal wreath
- Faux flowers

TOP TIP You could always swap out the glue gun for some wire to keep the florals in place so that you can reuse the metal wreath at some point.

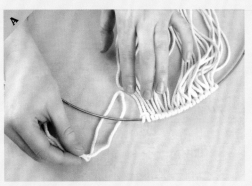

1 Plug in your glue gun to heat up.

2 Take the ball of macramé yarn, measure and cut twelve pieces of yarn measuring 50 inches each.

3 Pick up one of the pieces of yarn, fold it in half and place it underneath the metal wreath with the looped end directly in front of you and the two loose strands facing away **(step A)**.

4 Take the two loose strands and pull them towards you over the top of the metal wreath. Thread them through the looped end and pull the strand tightly to form a lark knot **(step B)**.

5 Repeat steps 3–4 to create lark knots with the rest of the strands **(step C)**.

6 Once all of the strands have been looped onto the metal wreath, place your finger on the two centre knots **(step D)**.

7 Take the first strand from the right-hand half and lay it across the left-hand side. Repeat with the closest strand on the left-hand side **(step E)**.

8 Repeat until all the strands have been crossed over **(step F)**.

9 Next, part the lark knots at the top and start to tie the pieces of macramé at the opposite side of the metal wreath, starting with the outer strands

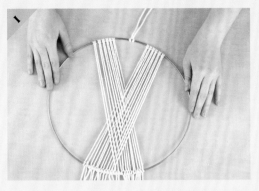

first and making sure to keep them crossed **(step G)**.

10 Repeat the knotting process until all of the strands are knotted on the wreath **(step H)**.

11 Cut another piece of macramé yarn, this time measuring 8 inches, and use it to create a lark knot hanging

at the top of the metal wreath **(step I)**.

12 Use your glue gun to adhere the flowers to the knotted end of the wreath, ensuring that all of the knotted pieces are covered with the flowers **(step J)**. Simply beautiful!

Marbled Mug

I first tried the marbling technique with ceramic baubles and coasters (some other great ways to use this technique). Then I thought about experimenting with a larger surface area and mugs seemed like a good next step!

It's really satisfying to create one-of-a-kind designs in this way but the added bonus is that you can give your creations to people as bespoke gifts. Your loved ones will be really impressed that you've made them something.

So, raid your cupboards, choose your nail varnishes and get started. It's a good idea to practise this technique ahead of time, so if you have an old mug that you don't mind experimenting with, give that a dip first!

You will need:

- Glass bowl (choose one you don't mind getting messy as the nail varnish sticks and can only be removed with nail varnish remover. It must be glass as other surfaces won't work – I speak from experience!)
- Kettle and water
- Nail varnish (select a few coordinating colours, if you like)
- Plain mug
- Rubber gloves (optional)
- A flat surface protected by some scrap paper

1   Fill your bowl two-thirds full with hot water. It needn't be boiling, but must be warm enough for the nail varnish to separate on the water's surface. Once the water is in the bowl, make sure you have all your items to hand, as you will need to work quite quickly **(step A)**.

2   Pour your nail varnishes gently onto the water, one at a time, in a circulate

motion to create swirls of colour on the water's surface **(steps B and C)**.

3   If you don't want to get nail varnish on your hands, pop on some rubber gloves. Holding the handle, dip your mug into the water submerging the outside of the mug into the nail varnish. **(step D)**.

4   Twist the mug around as you take it out of the water to create a swirling, marbled effect **(step E)**.

5   Set aside to dry for at least 15 minutes.

Painted Rock Photo Holder

I've used stones and rocks in a few different projects, but had to give this one a try as it's great to do with kids (if they're still little, maybe give them a hand with the wire!). To achieve the best results, the paint needs to dry for at least 24 hours, so this is a great weekend or holiday project.

I used Spectrum Noir Colorista paint markers for the fine-detail work and really enjoyed using them - such bright and vibrant shades!

TOP TIP These photo holders make great alternative Father's Day or Mother's Day gifts!

You will need:

- Medium-sized, smooth, clean rock
- Acrylic paint of your choice
- Paint marker pens (or more acrylic paints)
- Large paintbrush
- Small paintbrush (if using acrylic paint for the finer details)
- 20" aluminium craft wire
- Scissors
- Small photo

1   Paint the surface of your rock in your colour of choice then set aside to dry for 24 hours **(step A)**.

2   Give the rock a second coat of paint, if necessary, and set aside to dry for another 24 hours.

3   Using a different-coloured acrylic paint or a paint marker, start to outline and

fill in some shapes on the surface of the rock. Go for any design you like – as simple or as complex as you fancy. This is the time to let your creativity do the talking **(step B)**!

4   Once you're happy with your pattern, set aside to dry and have your wire ready **(step C)**.

5   When the rock is completely dry, take the wire and start to wrap it around the centre of the rock. Bind it enough times for it to feel secure **(step D)**.

6   Take the free end of the wire, lift it away from the rock and begin to coil it around one of your fingers. This will form the holder for your photo **(step E)**.

7   Once you are happy with the position of the holder, snip the end of the wire with some scissors.

8   Pop your chosen photo in place, and there you have it – a really fun and vibrant way to display precious memories!

Orange Drinks Tray

Nothing says summer like a juicy slice of fruit, and this showstopper of a drinks tray is the perfect way to serve a crisp gin and tonic on a gorgeous summer's day.

You'll also impress your friends and family when you tell them how you transformed a plain wooden tray into this bright and brilliant masterpiece!

TOP TIP   Why not create different fruit-themed trays with watermelon, lemon and passionfruit designs? Just switch out the paint and marker colours accordingly.

You will need:

- Circular wooden tray (the one shown here is 12" in diameter)
- Orange spray paint
- Medium-size paintbrush
- Light orange acrylic paint
- Yellow (or light orange), white and dark orange paint markers
- Spray sealant

1   Take the wooden tray and orange spray paint to a well-ventilated space – outside is best as it can get messy.

2   Spray the paint evenly over the tray, ensuring that it's fully covered. Leave outside to dry for 30 minutes **(step A)**.

3   Give the tray another coat of paint, if necessary, and leave to dry for 30 minutes.

4   Use your paintbrush and the light orange acrylic paint to create a border around the edge of the tray. The border should be a couple of inches thick **(step B)**.

5   Take the yellow paint marker to divide the tray into twelve equal sections.

Round them off slightly at the edges to create an orange segment effect **(steps C and D)**.

6   Using the white marker, add some white highlights to the edges of the segments **(step E)**.

7   Finally, take the dark orange paint marker and add some dots to the orange border **(step F)**.

8   Set aside to dry for a couple of hours before spraying a sealant over the board to add shine and to prevent the paint from chipping. Leave to dry as recommended by the instructions on the sealant before adding a couple of your favourite glasses and serving some refreshing drinks to your very impressed guests!

Ribbon Flowers

Who would have thought that you could use ribbons in this way? Pampas grass is such a popular home-décor item and this ribbon-pulling technique is such a clever way to recreate the trend.

You can customize the pieces by using any colours that you like. You could also make these flowers as big and as long as you like – simply switch out the standard wooden skewers for a larger size and add more pieces of ribbon to your red liner strips!

You will need:

- Three rolls of different shades of ribbon
- Scissors
- Red liner tape
- Wooden skewers
- Green floristry tape

TOP TIP Try not to tug on the ribbon too hard as you will most likely cause it to knot.

1   Cut three lengths, each measuring approximately 1½ inches, of each of the different-coloured ribbons. If you're using the same coloured ribbon, you will need nine pieces in total.

2   Roll out a length of red liner tape and attach the pieces of ribbon along it in a row **(step A)**.

3 Once all the pieces of ribbon are in place, take a small strand from each piece and pull it so that it frays.

4 Keep unravelling the ribbons, taking care to stop when you reach the red tape **(step B)**.

5 Next, peel off the red liner tape backing so you are left with the adhesive tape and the ribbons.

6 Take a wooden skewer and wrap the frayed-ribbon tape around it. Gradually work your way down the skewer as far as you can until you run out of tape **(step C)**.

7 To give the effect of a stalk, take a length of floristry tape and cover the remaining surface of the skewer in it.

8 Snip out some leaf shapes from another length of floristry tape and use the tape to stick them in place.

9 Repeat steps 1–8 to create a bunch of flowers then arrange them in your favourite small vase!

LED Découpage Candle

LED candles are a great way to increase the ambience of a room, especially when you can add an extra touch of personal style to them.

You wouldn't think that these stylish candles had been decorated using paper napkins – and literally any paper napkins will work – but they have! You can also use this technique to jazz up the surfaces of a variety of different items, including glass jars, ceramic vases, wooden trays and so much more.

You will need:

- Patterned paper napkins
- Mod Podge
- Medium-size paintbrush
- LED pillar candles of varying sizes
- Scissors

TOP TIP Try not to be too heavy handed with the glue as you may find that the ink in the design starts to bleed.

1 Take one of the paper napkins and carefully separate the patterned layer from the rest of the sheets.

2 Use your paintbrush to add a thin layer of Mod Podge to the surface of your first LED candle (step A).

3 Trying to keep the napkin in one piece, wrap it around the candle, press it into

place and smooth out any creases **(step B)**.

4 Once the napkin is in position and well adhered to the LED candle, brush a second thin layer of Mod Podge over the surface of the candle to seal the napkin in place **(step C)**.

5 Set the candle aside to dry for a few hours.

6 Once the Mod Podge is dry, take some scissors and trim the excess paper around the top of the candle to neaten things up.

7 Repeat steps 1–6 with your other candles, then place them on a side table, switch on and watch them glow!

Father's Day Gift

This probably won't come as much of a shock, but when it comes to Mother's Day or Father's Day, I love handmade gifts. Knowing how much joy I feel when I receive something completely handmade means that over the years I've helped the kids make all sorts of things for other people!

This Father's Day-inspired frame is the ideal last-minute gift. Dads and grandads will appreciate the personal touch, and the kids will love turning their dad into Superman (or any other superhero of your choice).

TOP TIP Personalize your figure and message for the special superhero in your family!

You will need:

- Glue gun
- Glue sticks
- 2 x stones (a smaller one for superhero head and a larger one for the body)
- Red and blue pens (ideally acrylic paint pens but good-quality felt tips should work just as well)
- Black fine liner
- Red felt or card (for cape)
- Scissors
- Box frame (the one used here is 6" x 6")
- White card
- Pencil and ruler

1   Plug in the glue gun to heat up.

2   Take your larger stone and use your acrylic paint marker or pen to colour it in blue with a bow design in red **(step A)**.

3   Take the smaller stone and use the black fine liner to draw a face on it.

4   Draw a cape proportional to the size of

the head and body onto your red card or felt. Cut this out and set aside with the two stones **(step B)**.

5   Remove the frame's backing, glass and paper insert.

6   Use the paper insert to measure an identical-sized piece of white card to fit comfortably inside the back of the frame.

7   Pop your piece of card back into the frame then use a pencil to sketch around the inside edges of the frame to identify your border. Once you have done this, you can remove the card and lay it on a flat surface.

8   Take your body and head stones, and card cape, then use the glue gun to adhere them to the centre of your card **(step C)**.

9   Using the black fine liner, write 'Super Dad' (or your chosen sentiment) along the top, taking care not to go outside of your pencil border line.

10 Next, use the pen to create a fun border. You can use a ruler if you like but freehand drawing adds to the cartoon-

style of the project. Using your coloured pens or acrylic paint markers, add some coloured dots to the background **(step D)**.

11 Place your card back into the frame, pop the frame backing in place again, then wrap your gift for Dad in time for the big day **(step E)**!

Shower Steamers

We've all heard of bath bombs and bath salts, but if you're not one for a long hot soak then shower steamers could be the perfect way to add a little bit of luxury to your self-care routine.

These little steamers are great to make as a batch. You can pick up a variety of different-shaped silicone moulds relatively easily and the finished items will look really nice stored in a glass jar in the bathroom.

TOP TIP Add the vodka to a small spray bottle. This will make it a lot easier to add it slowly to the mixture!

You will need:

- Rubber gloves (citric acid can irritate skin)
- ½ cup baking soda
- ¼ cup citric acid
- ¼ cup arrowroot powder
- Medium-size non-metallic bowl
- Non-metallic spoon (or just mix with your hands)
- 100 drops lemon oil
- 80 drops sweet orange oil
- 80 drops grapefruit oil
- Vodka
- Small spray bottle
- Silicone mould
- Lemon zest, to decorate

1   Put on your gloves and add the baking soda, citric acid and arrowroot to your non-metallic bowl. Mix together until well combined **(steps A and B)**.

2   Add the essential oils and stir thoroughly **(step C)**.

3   Start to pour or spray the vodka into the bowl. Work it into the contents of the

bowl until the mixture becomes the consistency of damp sand. It's really important that the mixture doesn't become too wet, or it will start to fizz prematurely **(step D)**.

4 When the mixture can be squeezed together and retains its shape, it's ready.

5 Sprinkle some of the lemon zest into the bottom of each of the moulds, then begin to fill with the mixture. Make sure to pack it down firmly.

6 Put the moulds in the fridge and leave to set for 24 hours. Carefully remove the shower steamers **(step E)**. Place in an airtight container until you're ready to enjoy them.

Pompom Mirror

Let me introduce you to the simplest of craft projects but one guaranteed to put a smile on your face! This bright and beautiful pompom mirror is ridiculously easy to make and you can upcycle an old mirror that you already have at home.

This project will add the perfect pop of colour to your getting-ready station or could make a really cute addition to a kid's bedroom or play area.

You will need:

- Glue gun
- Glue sticks
- Small pompoms (see page 26 for to make your own)
- Mirror

TOP TIP Switch out the rainbow-bright pompoms for more neutral tones if you'd like a completely different look and feel.

1 Plug in the glue gun to heat up.

2 Play around with the arrangement of the pompoms until you're happy, then fix them around the edges of the mirror using the glue gun **(steps A and B)**.

3 Set aside to dry for about an hour.

4 Brighten up a room with your brand-new mirror!

Flower Napkin Rings

These gorgeous napkin rings will add an instant pop of colour to any table setting and I love pairing them with colourful napkins to make them even jazzier. They're super simple, and a fantastic way to upcycle old curtain rings!

TOP TIP Keep a pair of scissors handy in case you need to trim any of the flowers or stems.

You will need:

- Glue gun
- Glue sticks
- Curtain rings
- Green floristry tape
- Scissors
- Faux flowers

1 Plug in the glue gun to heat up.

2 Take a curtain ring and bind floristry tape around it until it is completely covered, then tear or snip off the end **(steps A and B)**.

3 Using the glue gun, start to fix some faux blooms into the hook or hole at the top of the curtain ring **(step C)**.

4 Wrap some more floristry tape around the stems and bases of the flowers to cover any messy bits **(step D)**.

5 Set aside to dry for around 30 minutes.

6 Repeat steps 2–5 to create as many rings as you need, then add your napkins of choice. Pop on top of a plate setting for a summery spin to your table!

Gilded Wall Sconce

These beautiful wall hangings look great with dried flowers or blooms picked from the garden and will make any BBQ or afternoon with family and friends in an outside setting feel special. You can personalize them with any type of doorknob you like.

TOP TIP Tie a double knot in the rope hanging to make sure it's completely secure!

You will need:

- Plank of wood, approximately 12" x 4" x ½"
- Drill with drill bits
- Roll of jute rope
- White gesso
- 2 paintbrushes (one medium, one small)
- Gold gilding wax
- Screwdriver
- Twine
- Mason jar
- Doorknob of your choice

1   Drill two holes at the top of the wooden block, large enough to thread some jute rope through to create a hanging. Don't add the rope just yet.

2   Drill a third hole further down the wooden block and in the centre **(step A)**.

3   Mix some white gesso with a small amount of water, then use a medium-size paintbrush to apply this mixture to the surface of the wooden block. Set aside to dry for around 30 minutes. The intention is to create a distressed effect **(step B)**.

4   Use the small paintbrush to lightly paint some of the gold gilding wax over the wooden block once dry. Do so in streaks

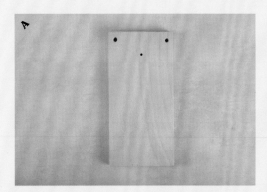

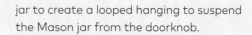

jar to create a looped hanging to suspend the Mason jar from the doorknob.

9   Add your chosen flowers to the glass jar then secure the loop of twine over the door knob.

10 Now, simply hang the sconce in your kitchen or on a wall outside for instant country chic!

to add to the distressed effect then set aside to dry **(step C)**.

5   Use a screwdriver to fasten the doorknob in place from the back of the wooden block **(step D)**.

6   Cut around 1½ feet of jute rope and thread it through the two top holes in the plank of wood to create a hanging. Tie each end off at the front so the knots are visible **(step E)**.

7   For the vase element, wrap a length of twine around the neck of the Mason jar multiple times. You'll probably need around 2 feet of twine. Snip the end and secure it in place using a bow.

8   Tie a third length of twine, around 1 foot in length, securely around the neck of the

Lemon Coasters

Create some show-stopping table accessories with these juicy lemon coasters! You'll find a macramé version of this coaster hack on page 122 but this fresh and fun alternative will look great under a glass of Pimm's or lemonade at a garden party or a summer BBQ.

You will need:

- Circle template (a large tin of tomatoes works well)
- Sticky-backed cork roll
- Scissors
- Pencil
- Ball of macramé cord
- Yellow acrylic paint
- Small paintbrush

TOP TIP Create a whole fruit basket of these gorgeous coasters – they would pair beautifully with the orange-inspired drinks tray on page 76.

1   Find a circular template that will be large enough to create your coaster shape.

2   Draw around your template onto the sheet of sticky-backed cork.

3   Cut out the shape with some scissors (**step A**).

4   Remove the plastic backing from the cork, keeping the sticky surface face up.

5   Find the centre of the cork circle and use your pencil to mark it with a small dot.

6   Press the end of your macramé cord over the dot and begin to wind it outwards in a spiral shape, pressing it firmly in place as you go **(step B)**.

7   Continue until your cord spiral covers the entire surface of the circle **(step C)**.

8   Take your acrylic paint and, using your paintbrush, create eight separate segments **(step D)**.

9   Next, paint a narrow border around the edge of the coaster to mimic the lemon peel **(step E)**.

10 Set aside to dry for a few hours.

11 Gather your favourite glassware and test out your new coasters!

Succulent Plant Pots

I'm always on the lookout for fun little projects that double as nice things to put around the house or in the garden (especially if you can do them with the kids). These little faux succulent pots fit the bill perfectly – all the more so because they'll last for ever! They're cute enough to stand on their own but if you use some acrylic paint markers to add your own bespoke designs, it takes things to a whole new level.

TOP TIP These little pots look best in sets of three!

You will need:

- Acrylic paint markers in various colours
- 3 miniature terracotta plant pots
- Scissors
- Cardboard (say from a cereal box) if the plant pots have a hole in their bottom
- Variety of faux succulents
- Sugar, sand or pebbles

1 Using your paint markers, draw a pattern or design onto each of your miniature plant pots. In my opinion, the bolder and brighter the better, but it's entirely up to you. This is the perfect step to rope the kids into helping with **(steps A and B)**.

2 Set aside to dry for 30 minutes.

3 With your scissors, cut a circle of cardboard the size of the base of your plant pots to block the hole if there is one; no need if not.

4 Add enough sand, sugar or pebbles – whatever you have to hand – to fill each pot. The level should sit ever so slightly below the rim so that it's not visible when you add your faux succulents.

5 Add 2–3 faux succulents to each pot and arrange them as you wish.

6 Place your pots on a table or window ledge for a warm desert vibe!

Hairband

Hairbands are a great way to add a bit of colour to brighten a mood and, let's face it, they're the perfect way to cover up a bad hair day!

This is a no-sew project so there's no need for any needles, thread or sewing skills. It's a no-fuss option to inject some personal style into your everyday look, and pretty soon you'll be making these for all your friends!

You will need:

- Glue gun (or fabric glue)
- Glue sticks
- Fabric of your choice
  (I used a 1' x 1' piece
  for this project)
- Plastic hairband
- Scissors

1   Plug in your glue gun (if using) to heat up.

2   Take your fabric and cut five strips approximately 8″ x 1½″ **(step A)**.

3   Select three of the strips and start plaiting them into a braid **(step B)**.

4   Apply some glue along the length of the hairband and wrap the fourth fabric strip around it until it is completely covered **(step C)**.

5   Trim the end of the fabric to neaten it up, but don't worry about it looking too perfect at this stage.

6   Place the finished braid across the top of the headband, glue into place and trim any excess fabric from each end **(step D)**.

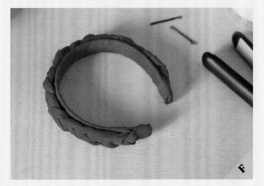

8   Once you're happy with the placement of the fabric, adhere it in place with the glue and leave to dry for 30 minutes **(step F)**. You're now ready to look FAB-U-LOUS.

7   Cut your final strip of fabric in half and use the two pieces to cover each end of the hairband. Take care to wrap the fabric around both the braid and the wrapped section of the band to hold everything in place **(step E)**.

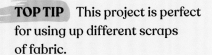

TOP TIP This project is perfect for using up different scraps of fabric.

DIY Air Freshener

Is there anything better than messing around with modelling clay? What a nostalgic throwback to school days! If it sounds like your idea of heaven, you're in for a treat.

Not only is this air freshener totally satisfying to make (it epitomizes crafting for wellness by putting our hands to work while we check out of our daily life for a little while) but the warm, terracotta tones also make for a modern and sophisticated style. Most importantly, the finished product will add the most gorgeous fresh scent to your bathroom, bedroom or car.

You will need:

- Air-drying terracotta clay
- Non-stick parchment paper
- Rolling pin
- Embossing folder (or piece of lace)
- Circular-shaped cookie cutter
- Straw (or alternative tool to make a similar-size hole)
- Macramé thread
- 2 wooden beads
- Comb
- Essential oil of your choice

TOP TIP The scent will fade over time so remember to top it up!

1   Cut a piece of clay a bit larger than a ping-pong ball and knead it to soften.

2   Lay a piece of non-stick parchment paper on your work surface and roll out the piece of clay to ¼ inch thick **(step A)**.

3   If using an embossing folder, make sure your piece of clay fits within the folder and doesn't overhang the sides. Or, if

6   Next, poke two holes through your circle shape, one at the top and one at the bottom, using your straw **(step E)**.

7   Set your clay circle aside to dry for 24–48 hours. You may need to turn the piece over every few hours to allow it to air-dry on both sides.

8   Once the piece of clay is completely dry, thread two separate lengths of thread through either hole, as well as a wooden bead onto each length **(step F)**.

9   Create a loop for hanging at one end and tie a knot in it to secure it. Then, tie a knot in the other length of thread but leave a short length of it free to become a tassel.

10 Use a comb or your fingers to separate the strands of thread to create a tassel.

11 Finish by adding a few drops of your favourite essential oil to the back of the disc.

12 Hang your finished piece in your bedroom, car, bathroom or wherever you like!

you're using a piece of lace, drape this over your piece of clay **(step B)**.

4   Use the rolling pin to impress the pattern. You'll need to apply a decent amount of pressure as you roll **(step C)**.

5   Take your cookie cutter and use it to cut out a circle from your clay **(step D)**.

Father's Day Shaker Card

Shaker cards are a great way to introduce a fun and interactive element to a handmade card. The sparkly 3D element, akin to a snowglobe, is a delight, and this particular design also enables you to add a personal touch with a photo of your choice.

Once you learn this technique, you can adapt it to a variety of different cards for various celebrations and occasions.

You will need:

- 12" x 8" white card, plus 4" x 3" for the frame
- Black card for mat and layer
- Patterned paper for mat and layer
- Scissors
- PVA glue
- Black fine liner
- Red liner tape
- Acetate measuring 5" x 4"
- Double-sided 3D foam strips
- Small photograph measuring 4" x 3"
- Sequins or confetti of your choice

1   Fold your white card in half to create a 6" x 4" tent-fold blank card. This means the fold is along the top rather than along the traditional left-hand side **(step A)**.

2   Layer up some black card and patterned papers on top of the blank card to create some neat mat and layers. Glue into place **(steps B and C)**.

3   Take your card rectangle measuring approximately 4" x 3". Cut out a square from inside, leaving a border of approximately half an inch at the top

and on both sides, making sure that your photo fits and is visible behind the frame. You should be left with a frame that resembles a Polaroid **(step D)**.

4   Take a black fine liner and write 'Happy Father's Day' along the bottom of the white card frame **(step E)**.

5   Use some red liner tape to adhere your acetate to the back of the frame to create a window **(step F)**.

6   Next, add strips of 3D foam along the top border and sides of the back of the frame. Then, add two further strips along the bottom border **(step G)**.

7   Tape around the card edges to ensure there are no gaps for the shaker pieces to escape through.

8   Sprinkle some sequins or confetti over the centre of your photograph.

9   Remove the backing plastic from the foam strips and position the frame directly over your photograph. Take care to press the strips firmly into place.

10 Glue your frame onto your card base and your shaker card is complete!

Glass Bauble Terrarium

These open glass baubles are widely available – I've seen them used for all sorts of things, including mini terrariums, Christmas-scene decorations and more. I think they make great outdoor decorations, especially during summer. Create half a dozen, hang them on your favourite tree or plant for a stunning feature in your blooming garden.

You will need:

- Set of open glass baubles
- Faux moss
- Faux foliage
- Faux flowers
- LED tealight (optional)
- Length of twine
- Scissors

TOP TIP You could put a festive spin on these baubles simply by adding some winter-themed foliage!

1 Start adding moss to the glass bauble. Add enough to create a decent base but don't overload the bauble too soon **(steps A and B)**.

2 Continue to build up your display by adding your chosen foliage and flowers. If you are including an LED tealight, remember to leave some space for it in the centre **(step C)**.

3 To create a hanging loop, take your length of twine and cut three long strands. Use the strands to fashion a plait, or simply use some strong ribbon or string that you have lying around **(steps D and E)**.

4 Thread the plait through the hole in the top of the glass bauble, then tie a knot in each of the ends.

5 Hang on the branch of a tree outside or on a hook in your home and admire!

Pressed Flower Frame

Dried and pressed flowers look so timeless and absolutely beautiful when presented in a glass frame. This is the perfect gift for someone special, and it will last a lifetime.

If you've been given some flowers, or have flowers in your garden or window box that you'd like to preserve, this is a creative way to keep them for yourself for even longer, or to give as a gift. Here's my easy, cheat's way to dry out your blooms in the microwave in just a few minutes!

You will need:

- Fresh flowers of your choice
- Hanging floating glass frame
- Scissors
- Paper
- Kitchen roll
- Microwave
- Tweezers

1   Trim your flowers to size so that they'll fit inside your frame. Fold a piece of paper in half and lay your flowers on top of it. It's important to lay them completely flat and separate from one another **(step A)**.

2   Place a piece of kitchen roll on top of the flowers.

3   Carefully place everything in the microwave then set a plate or bowl on top of the flowers to weigh them down.

4   Programme your microwave to the lowest setting and heat for 30 seconds. The flowers can take anywhere from

30 seconds to 5 minutes to dry out, depending on their moisture content, so continue to heat them in 30-second bursts, checking after each increment, until they feel dry and papery.

5   Open your frame and arrange the blooms on one side of the glass **(step B)**.

6   When you're happy with the look and feel of your design, close the frame securely and display or give as a gift!

TOP TIP If you're nervous about handling the dried flowers, use a pair of tweezers to arrange them in the frame.

Autumn

Sock Pumpkins

The great thing about crafting and creating is that once you've learned how to make something, you can use the finished piece in a variety of ways. Take these autumnal pumpkins, for example – they're cute enough to serve as standalone pieces as part of a table centrepiece, but you can also feature them in a wreath design, such as the one on the previous page.

So, if you like the look of these mini pumpkins, nail the technique first then enjoy using them in all sorts of creative ways!

You will need:

- Glue gun
- Glue sticks
- Socks
- Scissors
- Hair doughnuts
- Twine
- Cinnamon sticks

1   Plug in your glue gun to heat up.

2   Take one of the socks and cut off the toe section **(step A)**.

3   Feed the sock through the centre of the hair doughnut. Make sure there is enough sock to feed back over the top **(step B)**.

4   Pull the shorter section of sock back over the doughnut **(step C)**.

5   Feed the sock through the centre again and repeat **(step D)**.

6   The hair doughnut should now be completely covered with material and you should have a neat finish **(step E)**.

7 Cut six lengths of twine, approximately 6 inches each.

8 Loop each length of twine around the hair doughnut in equally spaced sections then tie them off underneath **(step F)**.

9 Turn the hair doughnut over. The top side should look neat and your pumpkin design should be starting to shape up **(step G)**.

10 Use your glue gun to bond a couple of cinnamon sticks together. These will give your pumpkin a very cute stalk effect.

11 Fix the cinnamon sticks into the centre of the doughnut and there you have it – a stylish autumnal pumpkin fit for any sideboard or table centrepiece.

Autumnal Wreath

I love the colours that autumn brings – all the oranges, greens, yellows, browns and reds. There are so many vibrant tones and shades to play with, especially when it comes to crafting and home décor. So, here's another great wreath, inspired by the fantastic colours of this beautiful season, to add to your collection. You may have spotted that this one features another craft from page 108.

features another craft from page 108.

You will need:

- Glue gun
- Glue sticks
- 4 sock pumpkins from page 108
- Willow wreath base
- Faux foliage
- A few pine cones
- Ribbon (roughly 3')

TOP TIP Play around with the placement of your pumpkins and faux foliage before adhering everything into place.

1 Create four sock pumpkins of varying sizes from page 108.

2 Plug in your glue gun to heat up.

3 Using the glue gun, stick the pumpkins to one half of the wreath. Setting the pumpkins at different angles will make the wreath look much more interesting, so rather than placing them equally, turn

some inwards and outwards, and have some positioned slightly underneath **(step A)**.

4   Next, stick the faux foliage and the pine cones into place around the pumpkins. Again, try to set the pine cones at different angles and intervals, and use the foliage to fill in the gaps, making sure the bottom half of the wreath is completely covered **(steps B and C)**.

5   Set aside to dry for at least 30 minutes.

6   Cut your ribbon in half and tie it around the top half of the wreath to create a loop **(step D)**.

7   Next, tie a bow, trim the trailing ends and glue into place on top of the ribbon loop **(step E)**.

8   Hang your autumnal showstopper on your front door!

Floating Ghosts

Sometimes the simplest things have the most impact, which can definitely be said of these floating Halloween ghosts. With nearly 1.5 million views on social media, this project is still my most-loved viral craft video and it's easy to see why!

I absolutely love making them because they always get such a great reaction. They're simple to pull together and are pretty much hassle-free (which is ideal if you're looking for a last-minute Halloween decoration to do with the kids).

TOP TIP Hold on to any drinks cups you pick up from fast-food restaurants – they make the perfect-sized holders for the ghosts to dry on. You won't have to worry about getting any fabric stabilizer on your good glasses or cups either!

You will need:

- Party balloon
- Large plastic or cardboard tumbler
- Muslin fabric (please account for the need to double if using thin muslin per instructions, and for the length of ghost, so between 3' and 6' square)
- Scissors
- Large plastic tray
- Fabric stabilizer spray
- Black marker pen

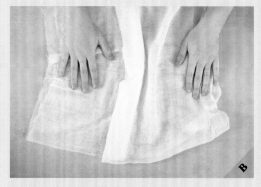

1   Inflate a balloon so that it is large enough to sit just inside the rim of a large plastic or cardboard tumbler **(step A)**.

2   Place your balloon-and-cup structure upright on a flat surface.

3   Take your piece of muslin fabric. If it's very thin, you may need to double the layers used **(step B)**.

4   Drape your muslin over the top of the balloon and cup to see how the fabric falls – the bottom of it should skim your work surface ever so slightly **(step C)**.

5   Make sure you are happy with the fabric
length. Trim any excess, if necessary
(step D).

6   Remove the fabric from the balloon and
transfer it to your plastic tray (the fabric
stabilizer contains starch and will make
the surface sticky).

7   Drench the muslin in fabric stabilizer so
that it is wet but not dripping **(step E)**.

8   Drape the wet fabric back over the top
of your balloon-and-cup structure and
leave it to dry for 24 hours.

9   Once completely dry, give your spooky
friend some eyes and a mouth, using
a black permanent marker, and hey
presto, your ghoulsome ghost is
Halloween ready.

Hessian Pumpkins

Who says pumpkins are just for Halloween? I really enjoy adding autumnal touches to my house and these cute pumpkins are a really grown-up take on the home-décor trend.

1 Plug in your glue gun to heat up.

2 Scrunch the bits of padding into a ball shape. An outer layer of bubble wrap is useful to hold everything together **(step A)**.

3 Use your scissors to cut a square of hessian fabric large enough to accommodate the ball of padding **(step B)**.

You will need:

- Glue gun
- Glue sticks
- Padding (newspaper, bubble wrap, tissue paper – you name it!)
- Scissors
- Hessian fabric
- Twine
- Cinnamon sticks
- Raffia ribbon
- Autumnal faux foliage
- Star anise

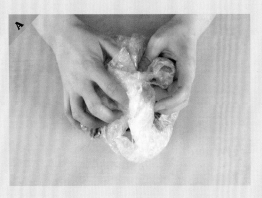

4 Set the ball of padding in the middle of your hessian square. Draw the corners of the fabric into the centre, adding a small amount of glue each time to keep the material in place **(step C)**.

5 Cut a length of twine long enough to wrap around the pumpkin, then tie and knot in place. Take care to ensure that when you tie the knot, it's on the

underside of the pumpkin where you have glued the hessian into place **(step D)**.

6 Repeat step 5 to form a cross shape with the twine, then repeat a further two times on either side to form a pumpkin shape **(step E)**.

7 Make sure all of the ties are neat and secure on the underside of the pumpkin then turn it over to face the right way up.

8 Take 2–3 cinnamon sticks and bind them together with a length of raffia ribbon.

9 Use your glue gun to fix the cinnamon sticks to the centre of the pumpkin.

10 Take some faux leaves and star anise, and glue in place around the cinnamon sticks **(step F)**.

11 Set aside to dry for 30 minutes then repeat steps 2–10 to make as many pumpkins as you wish.

12 Arrange your finished pumpkins on a table with some candles as the perfect autumnal touch to a room!

Witch's Broom Treat Bag

Halloween is a really great time to get creative because there are tons of different projects to experiment with – cards, decorations, costumes and so many more. I for one absolutely love looking for new ideas each year.

These witchy-themed treat bags are fantastic to make with kids (as long as the younger ones are supervised while they use scissors). They make the most fabulous little party bags for a spooktacular Halloween party, or for any little monsters who come trick or treating at your door.

TOP TIP Two pairs of hands make this project a lot easier, especially when trying to tie the two treat bags together – that's the tricky part!

You will need:

- Two brown paper bags
- Scissors
- Treats (to put into the bag)
- Wooden dowel or stick
- Brown felt-tip pen or paint
- Raffia
- Ribbon

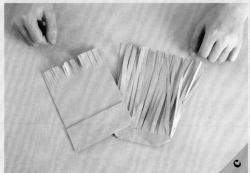

1   Take one of the paper bags, push out its base and fold in both sides **(step A)**.

2   Cut a series of narrow strips all the way down to the base line of the bag **(step B)**.

3   With the second bag, cut some more strips, roughly an inch long, at the top of the bag **(step C)**.

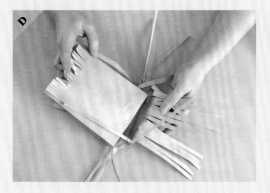

4   Place the second bag inside the first and fill with treats **(see step D)**.

5   If you're using a wooden dowel instead of a stick, take a brown felt-tip pen or some brown paint and colour the surface of the dowel until three-quarters of its length is covered. This will give it a broom-handle-like finish **(step E)**.

6   Slip the dowel or stick into the centre of the bags to create the broom handle.

7   Gather the strips together and cinch them at the top. Secure them in place around the dowel/stick with a length of raffia tied in a knot and finished with a ribbon bow **(step F)**.

Plant Pot Gonk

My dad has an allotment and we have a little greenhouse in our garden, so our kids are constantly outside, planting little bits, watering, and harvesting lots of home-grown fruit and veg. They adore it and I think it's so important for kids to know where things come from.

Anyway, this wee garden gonk would make such a cute decoration for an outdoor area or the perfect little gift for someone with green fingers!

You will need:

- Glue gun
- Glue sticks
- Ball of wool
- Pompom-making tool
- Wooden bead or ball
- Miniature plant pot
- Twine
- Small piece of autumnal faux foliage

TOP TIP For ease, make sure your miniature plant pot has a pre-drilled hole in the bottom.

1   Plug in your glue gun to heat up.

2   Use your wool and pompom making tool to create a medium-sized pompom as shown on page 26 **(step A)**.

3   Using a dab of glue from the glue gun, stick a wooden bead or ball to the centre of the pompom **(step B)**.

4 Cut a length of twine (roughly 12 inches) and fold it in half **(step C)**.

5 Tie the loose ends together in a knot large enough not to slip through the hole in the bottom of the plant pot, then thread the looped end through the plant-pot hole to create a hanging **(step D)**.

6 Use the glue gun to run a line of adhesive round the inner rim of the plant pot.

7 Add the pompom to the plant pot and push into place so that it sticks to the glue well **(step E)**.

8 Finally, glue a small piece of autumnal foliage to the front of the plant pot and your curious little creature is complete **(step F)**!

Clay Trinket Tray

I love air-dry clay and have made so many things with it. It's especially fun to use with the kids to create memorable keepsakes. I remember how years ago you had to buy clay that needed to go in the oven, but these days it's all air-dry and hassle-free.

This trinket tray is a great starter project for anyone new to the product. I still keep my tray on my make-up stand so that my rings, earrings and other bits and bobs are all in one place!

You will need:

- Air-dry clay
- Knife
- Rolling pin
- Acrylic paints in various colours
- Small paint brushes

TOP TIP Try not to roll the clay out too thin – you don't want it to become brittle when dry.

1 Cut a piece of clay about the size of a satsuma **(step A)**.

2 Roll it out so that it's roughly the size and shape of an envelope and around half an inch in thickness.

3 Trim the edges with your knife to create a neat rectangle.

4 Using your fingers, mould the sides of the tray upwards to give it a slightly raised rim **(step B)**.

5 When you're happy with the overall look of your tray, set it aside to dry for around 24 hours.

6 Once the clay is completely dry, it's time to paint! Take your first acrylic

like this to be perfectly straight, use a ruler. Then, paint one half of the tray in your chosen colour.

7   Next, take a second paint colour and, using a fresh paint brush, gently spatter some paint across the entire tray **(step C)**.

8   Set aside to dry for at least 1 hour.

9   Once dry, add your favourite pieces of jewellery to your stylish new trinket dish!

colour and mark a diagonal line across the tray, from corner to corner. If you'd

Macramé Coasters

I'm a huge fan of these boho-chic coasters – they're the perfect example of how brilliant it can be to make your own home-décor pieces. No one would know that you'd made them yourself but they'd be all the more impressed by it.

Not only do these coasters look fabulous but they're also a cheat's way of experimenting with the techniques and many knots that can be involved with macramé. What a great introduction to this stylish trend!

You will need:

- Glue gun
- Glue sticks
- Circle template
- Pencil
- Scissors
- Self-adhesive cork sheet
- Macramé or cotton cord
- Comb

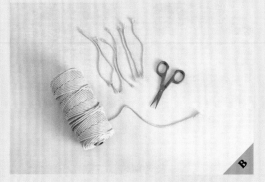

1 Plug in your glue gun to heat up.

2 Use your template to cut a circle out of the self-adhesive cork sheet.

3 Turn the cork circle over so that its sticky side is facing upwards. Find the centre of the circle and mark it with a pencil.

4 Peel off the adhesive backing and place the end of your macramé cord on the centre point of the circle.

5 Start to spiral the macramé cord outwards until the adhesive base of the cork is covered. Leave a small border around the edge for a final coil of cord and the macramé tassels **(step A)**.

6 Measure out how much more macramé cord you will need to go once more around the circle but do not press this down onto the adhesive backing. This will form your border piece in due course.

7 Cut some smaller lengths of macramé cord. You'll need around 50 pieces, measuring about 5–6 inches each, depending on how long you'd like your tassels to be **(step B)**.

8   Begin to tie each smaller length of cord to your border piece using a cow-hitch knot. To create a cow-hitch knot, fold one of the 5-inch pieces of cord in half and lay it over the border piece so that the looped end is at the top and the loose ends are at the bottom. Next, take the loose ends and thread them through the looped end, passing underneath the border string to do so. Pull to form the knot **(steps C, D and E)**.

9   Repeat step 8 until the entire border piece has been covered then press this into place on the adhesive cork backing.

10 Use the comb or your fingers to separate the strands of macramé cord and create a tasselled effect **(step F)**. Simply gorgeous!

Rope Tray

Beautiful centrepieces are just as popular as they have ever been. I've tried a few different projects to create the perfect centrepiece tray and this boho chic-inspired piece has to be one of my favourites. It looks effortlessly stylish and really is straightforward to make.

The best piece of advice I can give to you for this project is not to throw away your old Christmas charger plates! One of them is the perfect size to upcycle into this gorgeous tray. Just add some candles and you're good to go.

TOP TIP Try not to overdo it with the glue. Use only what you need because if you use too much, it will end up being visible.

You will need:

- Glue gun
- Glue sticks
- Charger plate (or old circular tray that you're happy to upcycle)
- Thick rope
- Scissors
- Wooden rings (I used 25 wooden curtain rings)

1   Plug in your glue gun to heat up.

2   Take the rope and use the glue gun to adhere it to the centre of the tray.

3   From the centre starting point, spiral the rope outwards, gluing it into place as you go (**step A**).

4   Once the plate is completely covered

with the rope, cut it at an appropriate point with some sharp scissors **(step B)**.

5   Set aside to dry.

6   Once the rope is glued firmly in place, use the glue gun to adhere all of the wooden rings to the outer edge of the

tray on top of the rope. Take care not to use too much glue **(step C)**.

7   Set aside to dry.

8   Style your finished tray with candles and ornaments of your choosing. Beautiful!

Dried Flower Hanging

As you'll have discovered by now, I love experimenting with dried flowers! I couldn't resist sharing another beautiful way to use and display them in your home. If you're looking to give someone flowers, this dried arrangement would also serve as a perfect alternative to fresh blooms as it will last a lifetime.

You can press the flowers yourself or buy them ready-dried then arrange them however you like. You could also switch out the flowers to suit any season.

TOP TIP When you're wrapping the twine around the ring, make sure it's taut enough to keep the flowers in place but not so tight that you can't slot them into position!

You will need:

- Ball of brown twine
- Metal hoop
- Scissors
- Dried flowers

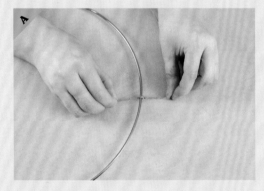

1. Tie the free end of your brown twine to one side of the metal hoop **(step A)**.

2. Next, wrap the twine around the hoop repeatedly to form a band across its centre.

3. When the band is thick enough to slot your flowers into it, snip the twine free from the ball and tie it to the hoop to secure it **(step B)**.

4. Weave your dried flowers in between the sections of twine in a style to suit **(step C)**.

5. Add a small twine bow to the right-hand side of the band of twine **(step D)**.

6. Tie a loop of string at one end of the hoop for hanging, secure it with a knot then step back and admire your handiwork!

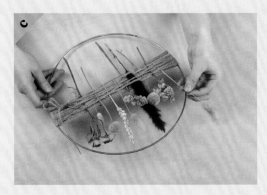

Wooden Ball Candle Holder

I don't know about you but I adore the Scandi interiors vibe and love adding pieces to my home that have been inspired by this laid-back look. I love it even more when I'm able to create something myself instead of spending lots of money on shop-bought items! The feeling when someone asks you where you've bought something from, only for you to turn around and say you made it yourself, never gets old!

You will need:

- Glue gun
- Glue sticks
- 27 large wooden craft beads
- 9 white taper candles
- Table knife

TOP TIP If your candles don't quite fit into the holes in the beads, use a table knife to carve some of the wax from the bottom of each candle to narrow it.

1 Find a clear and even surface to work on. You'll need to keep the base of your structure perfectly flat while you're gluing the different pieces together.

2 Plug in your glue gun to heat up.

3 Take one of the wooden beads and adhere it to another sideways on, so that the tops of the beads and their holes are facing up.

4 Continue to create your base for the candle holder. To do this, glue nine of the wooden beads together in a 3 x 3 structure, following the technique in step 3 **(step A)**.

5 Set your base to one side to dry and create a further two of these 3 x 3 structures.

6 Once all three of the 3 x 3 structures are dry and feel sturdy, stack them on top of one another and glue them into place.

7 Set aside to dry for 30 minutes.

8 Add your candles and find a suitable spot for your new home-décor piece!

Glue Gun Canvas

Creating home-décor pieces is one of my favourite things to do, and there's nothing better than seeing something you like in a shop or in a magazine then being able to recreate it at home. This technique couldn't be easier to perfect but, as you can see, the end result is gorgeous!

TOP TIP Have plenty of glue sticks to hand for this project – you'll need them!

You will need:

- Glue gun
- Spare glue sticks
- Stretched canvas in a size of your choosing
- Metallic paint marker in your chosen colour

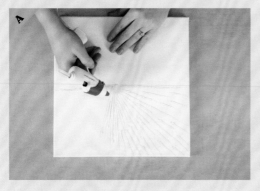

1 Plug in your glue gun to heat up and place your canvas in front of you.

2 Once the glue gun is hot enough, start to squeeze the glue onto your canvas, creating multiple beads stretching outwards from the centre point **(step A)**. Remember – there's no perfect result, each design is unique!

3 When you are happy with your design, set your canvas to one side to dry.

4 Once the glue is dry, take your metallic marker and colour the raised design. Be careful not to get any marker on the canvas itself **(step B)**.

5 Set aside to dry again for 30 minutes **(step C)**.

6 Once fully dry, hang your work of art in your chosen spot!

Bird Feeder

Autumn is a great time to put a little something extra out for the birds, and this really simple project is a fantastic way to recycle toilet-roll tubes and ice-lolly sticks. It's also a good one to get the kids involved with – they'll have lots of fun adding the peanut butter and seeds to the cardboard tube, and even more fun when they see the birds enjoying their homemade snack in the garden!

You will need:

- Knife
- Toilet- or kitchen-roll tube
- Mixed bird seed
- Plate
- Peanut butter
- 2 wooden ice-lolly sticks
- Twine
- Scissors

TOP TIP Save up ice-lolly sticks from summertime to use in this craft!

1   Take a knife and create four holes at one end of your toilet-roll tube, two on either side, which will be for the lolly sticks.

2   At the other end of the tube, punch two corresponding holes on either side which will be for the twine loop **(step A)**.

3   Take the packet of bird seed and sprinkle a good layer of it onto your plate.

4   Next, use your knife to spread a thin layer of peanut butter over the surface of the toilet-roll tube **(step B)**.

5   Roll the tube in the bird seed **(step C)**.

6   Cut a length of twine and tie it securely to the end of the toilet-roll tube with two holes on either side.

7   Next, flip the cardboard tube around so that you're looking at the end with four holes.

8   Pick up a lolly stick and push it through one of the holes on the side nearest to you, and then out through the corresponding hole on the other side.

9 Repeat with the second stick and other two holes so that the two sticks cross over each other **(step D)**.

10 Hang your bird feeder on a branch outside and enjoy watching your feathered friends tuck into something tasty and filling.

Macramé Feathers

These beautiful macramé feathers make for an absolutely stunning wall display, especially when hung on rustic wooden sticks and arranged with a whole bunch of different-sized feathers.

I will admit that although it might take a couple of goes to perfect the technique, fashioning the knots, brushing out the strands and then trimming each piece to create an individual feather is extremely satisfying!

You will need

- Macramé cord
- Scissors
- Tape
- Brush or comb
- Fabric stiffener
- Wooden stick or dowel

TOP TIP Alter the length of the cords used in this project to create a variety of different-sized feathers.

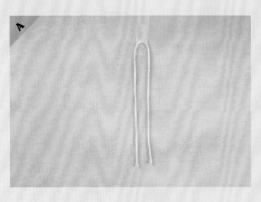

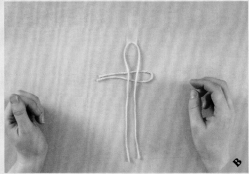

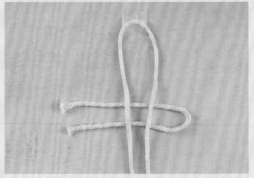

1   Cut one 16-inch length of macramé cord, ten 10-inch lengths and eight 8-inch lengths of cord.

2   Take the 16-inch length and fold it in half. Tape the folded end to your surface to hold it into place for ease **(step A)**.

3   Next, take one of the 10-inch strands and tuck it under the main length **(step B)**.

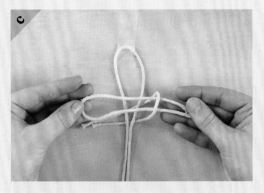

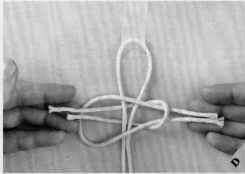

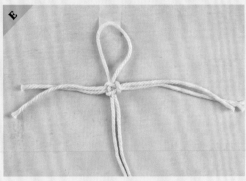

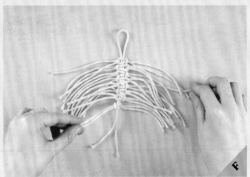

4   Take another 10-inch strand and pull the looped end through the looped strand underneath the main length **(step C)**.

5   Take the loose strands of the first loop and tuck these through the second loop that's draped across the main strand **(step D)**.

6   Take the loose strands of each end in your hands and pull to create your first knot **(steps D and E)**.

7   Repeat steps 3–6 but alternate the side on which you create the knots. Use up all of the 10-inch lengths of cord before you make your way onto using the 8-inch lengths. Do this so that the feather shape tapers at the bottom **(step F)**.

8   Work towards the bottom of the main strand until you have a couple of inches of cord left **(step G)**.

9   Make sure all of your knots are tightened up then start to brush out the individual strands with your brush or comb **(step H)**.

10 Spray your feather with some fabric stiffener and set aside to dry.

11 Use a pair of scissors to trim the edges of the feather to create a neater and more distinct shape **(step I)**.

12 Loop your feather through a wooden stick or dowel to display.

TOP TIP Use hairspray if you don't have any fabric stabilizer to hand.

TOP TIP These feathers also make great keyrings – simply reduce the length of the strings and the number of knots you create for each piece.

Citronella Candle

There's nothing better than making the most of what's left of those warmer evenings outdoors with a couple of drinks, some blankets and a good old natter. The only thing that's missing from that scenario is a couple of gorgeous-smelling candles to keep away any unwanted beasties and add a lovely bit of ambience!

You will need:

- 7oz medium-size glass jar (a jam jar, for example)
- Weighted candle wick and sticky tab (these usually come together in a pack)
- Wick-centering tool
- 5oz wax pellets
- Melting pot
- Medium-size saucepan
- Thermometer
- Something for stirring the wax
- 5–6 drops citronella oil
- Ribbon (optional)

1 Add the wick to the base of your glass jar, using the tab, and thread the wick through the centering tool (steps A and B).

2 Weigh out 5oz wax pellets to make a candle for an average-sized jam jar.

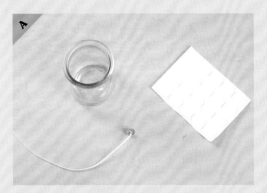

3 Add the wax pellets to the melting pot.

4 Fill your saucepan with hot water roughly an inch deep. Make sure the water is not boiling and doesn't exceed 92°F so as not to spoil the wax.

5 Set the melting pot on the rim of the saucepan, resting above the hot water (step C).

6 Keep checking on the temperature of the water as the wax begins to melt.

7 Just before the wax has completely melted, add 5–6 drops of the citronella oil and stir well (**step D**).

8 Turn off the heat and let the wax cool for a few minutes.

9 Gently decant the wax into your jar, making sure to keep the wick centred. Stop when the wax is nearly at the rim of the jar, then set aside to cool fully (**step E**).

10 As an optional extra, tie a length of ribbon around the neck of the jar as a beautiful finishing touch.

Rope Basket

The aesthetic of this rope basket is wonderfully rustic and will bring so much charm to a kitchen or dining area as a standalone piece. It's a lazy-afternoon sort of project, and once you've made one, you could switch out the rope and fabric to create others.

This versatile basket can be used as a planter, or as a pretty solution to storing those random bits and bobs we find all over the house!

TOP TIP Take care not to glue your fabric to your plastic container as you'll slip this out once you've used it to shape your basket.

You will need:

- Glue gun
- Glue sticks
- Cylindrical plastic container
- Fabric (a piece large enough to wrap around the container completely)
- Rope
- Scissors
- Ribbon
- White card
- Pencil

1   Plug in your glue gun to heat up.

2   Smooth out your fabric on a flat table or surface and place the container in the centre (**step A**).

3   Wrap the fabric around the sides of the container until the two edges of fabric meet and slightly overlap (**step B**).

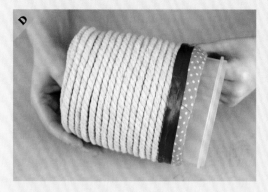

4   Use the glue gun to bond the two edges of fabric together but do not stick them to the plastic container.

5   Next, fold the two pieces of fabric underneath the base of the container and glue them to one another, almost as if you're wrapping a present.

6   Tuck any excess fabric inside the plastic container **(step C)**.

7   Turn the container over so that you're looking at the base again. Take your length of rope and start to spiral it out from the centre of the container's base, gluing it in place as you go.

8   Continue to coil the rope and glue it in place until you have covered the base and the sides of the container.

9   Set aside to dry for 30 minutes.

10 Once the glue is dry, place one hand inside the container and use it to gently draw the container out so that you're left with a rope-and-fabric container/basket **(step D)**.

11 Fold the fabric over the top of the rope section and trim with scissors, if needed.

12 Take a length of ribbon and glue it around the circumference of the basket, over the fabric's edge.

13 To improve the sturdiness of the rope basket, take your white card and draw a circle shape large enough to fit inside the bottom of the container. Cut it out and pop it into place **(step E)**.

All done!

Winter

Christmas Garland or Wreath

One of my favourite memories and Christmas traditions from when I was a kid is getting all wrapped up and heading down to a frosty riverbank in Durham with my mam and sister. We'd forage holly and berries from the hedgerows then take our goodies home and use them to create our own festive garlands and wreaths.

This project is all about upcycling and breathing new life into what you might already have at home. You can even keep the same garland base and spruce it up each year with different combinations of holly, pine cones, decorations, and even twinkling lights!

You will need:

- Plain faux garland
- Craft wire or floristry wire

To decorate:
- Dried orange and/ or cinnamon slices (optional)
- Baubles
- Pine cones
- Holly and berries
- Winter foliage picks
- Battery-operated fairy lights (optional)
- Zip ties
- Hook, hammer and nail (optional)

1 Lay out your garland and separate your decorations into piles.

2 If you're using fairy lights, wind them around the garland, making sure you have an even spread of lights.

3 Time for some decorations! Focus on the arrangement of your trimmings first, and work in groups of three. Gather a trio of decorations at a time and make sure to space them evenly along your garland **(steps A and B)**.

4 To secure the decorations in place, loop a piece of craft or floristry wire through each one, twist the two ends together, then wrap the wire around the garland. Arrange any greenery around the decorations to make sure the wire isn't too visible.

5 Continue until your garland looks just right. Then, if you want to turn it into a beautiful wreath for your front door, simply use some more wire or a zip tie to join the two ends together. Add a nail or a hook to your door, if necessary, or hang your wreath from your door knocker, if you have one. Otherwise, it's time to drape your garland over the mantelpiece, stand back and admire it.

Decorated Ceramic Baubles

Ceramic baubles are so versatile – they are the perfect base for a creative project such as this, and the design possibilities are endless. Using just some acrylic paint markers, which also come in handy for so many other crafting activities, you can completely transform these basic baubles into luxury-looking festive decorations to adorn your Christmas tree. It's a great craft to involve older kids and teenagers in too!

Take a look at the three different designs I've used for these baubles. They should give you some ideas to get started, but you can really let your creativity run wild!

You will need:

- Pencil
- Paper
- Plain ceramic baubles
- Acrylic paint markers in a variety of colours

TOP TIP The marbling technique on page 72 is also incredibly effective on ceramic baubles!

1   For a practice run, use a pencil to sketch your chosen design onto some paper.

2   If you're still a little hesitant about mapping your design directly onto your ceramic bauble using the pens, use your pencil to lightly sketch it out first **(step A)**.

3   Go over your design with the marker pens **(step B)**.

It really is that simple!

No-sew Christmas Bag

There are so many ways to wrap and present gifts at Christmas, but more than ever, as a population, we aim to use materials that can be recycled and reused. Recyclable wrapping paper is now widely available, but you can also use fabric to wrap presents, and that's where these cute little bags come in.

As their name suggests, these no-sew gift bags require zero stitching, and they're really simple but durable. What's more, they don't require a lot of fabric, so you can use up any scraps of material that you have to hand.

You will need:

- Iron
- Two fabric rectangles measuring 11" x 8" each
- Ruler
- Fabric/textile glue
- Ribbon
- Small safety pin
- Scissors

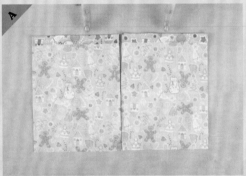

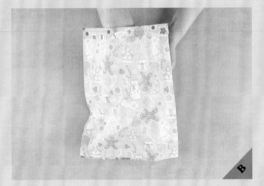

1   Plug in your iron to heat up.

2   Set your fabric pieces in front of you with the 8-inch sides at the top and bottom, non-printed side face up. Measure 1 inch from the top of each piece of fabric then fold over to this point. Iron to create a sharp crease then open the fold back up.

3   Add a thin line of glue along the top edge of the fabric. Fold the material down by an inch and press it firmly in place, being careful to preserve the gap

in between the two layers of fabric for the ribbon drawstring to run through **(step A)**.

4   Repeat step 3 on the second piece of fabric and set aside to dry for about 30 minutes.

5   Once the glue is dry, turn one of the pieces of fabric over so that the non-printed side is face down. Add a line of textile glue down either side and along the bottom edge. Then, take the other piece of fabric and lay it over the first piece – this time non-printed side face up. Press firmly in place. You should now be looking at the non-printed side or inside of the bag **(step B)**.

6   Set aside to dry for 30 minutes.

7   Next, it's time to add the ribbon drawstring. You can add two separate lengths of ribbon to either side of your bag or use one long piece and thread it through both sides of the bag.

8   For either option, take your safety pin and attach it to one end of your ribbon. Use the pin to move the ribbon through either side of your top folded section **(steps C and D)**.

9   Once complete, either tie off the ends of the long piece of ribbon or tie both

ends of your separate pieces of ribbon together **(steps E and F)**.

10 Turn your bag inside out, fill it with festive goodies and you're ready to give as a gift!

Candy-cane Santa Place Settings

I don't know about you, but I pick up a box of candy canes every Christmas and use them for all sorts – including festive crafting. These Santa-themed candy-cane place settings are a fun activity to try with the kids. They're super easy to make a couple of days beforehand, look fantastic, and you can also snack on them later in the day when the Christmas pudding has settled!

TOP TIP   Add a little hot glue to the centre of the three candy canes to hold them in place if you're having trouble keeping them sturdy (and aren't bothered about having a bit of an after-dinner snack!).

You will need:

- 3 candy canes (per place setting)
- Ribbon
- Scissors
- Ruler
- Red card
- Black card
- Gold card
- Glue tape pen
- Black fine liner

1   Take three candy canes and arrange them so that two are pointing towards the front and one is supporting the others in the back.

2   Cut a length of ribbon and tie all three candy canes together in this same position **(step A)**.

3   Cut a piece of red card measuring 2" x 3", a rectangular piece of black card measuring ½" x 3", a square piece measuring ½" x ½" and a piece of gold card measuring 1" x 1" **(step B)**.

4   Take the rectangular piece of black card and run your glue tape pen across the back of it, then position this piece of card along the bottom third of the piece of red card **(step C)**.

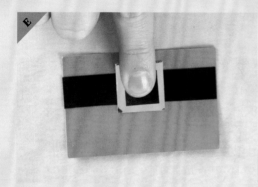

5   Next, add some adhesive to the back of the square piece of gold card and stick this card in the centre of the black strip **(step D)**.

6   Roll a strip of glue onto the final piece of black card – the small square – and add it to the centre of the gold square to finish the Santa's-belt look **(step E)**.

7   Finally, write your guest's name onto the piece of card with the black fine liner **(step F)** then tuck it into the crooks of the two front-facing candy canes.

8   Make as many place settings as you have guests and arrange on your Christmas table in time for the big day!

Snow-effect Jars

Create an enviable snowy scene on your dining-room table with these gorgeous snow-effect jars! They are a doddle to make using glass jars, and the best thing is that you'll probably already have the main component in your bathroom . . . Epsom salts!

You will need:

- Glue gun
- Glue sticks
- Length of scrap paper to protect your work surface
- A few handfuls of Epsom salts
- Permanent spray adhesive
- 2 glass jars or vases of different sizes
- Twine
- 2 faux Christmas picks
- 2 sets battery-operated fairy lights

TOP TIP Don't use too much adhesive on your jars or the salts will start to dissolve.

1 Plug in your glue gun to heat up.

2 Scatter the Epsom salts over the paper on your chosen work surface **(step A)**.

3 Cover your first jar or vase in spray adhesive and roll it across the layer of Epsom salts, making sure that its surface is fully covered **(steps B and C)**.

4 Set it aside to dry for 30 minutes.

5 Once the jar is dry, plug in the glue gun to heat up.

6 Take a length of twine and wrap it around the neck of the jar or vase. Tie it off in a bow. Glue the twine into place **(step D)**.

7   Take a faux Christmas pick and use the glue gun to fix it to the front of the jar.

8   Set aside to dry then repeat steps 3–7 with your second jar.

9   Add a string of fairy lights to each jar and place in the centre of your table ready for the big day!

Paper Bag Snowflakes

These snowflakes are super simple to make but they always have a huge impact, especially when people find out that all they need to make them are some plain paper bags! For the ultimate festive scene, make a set of different-sized snowflakes and hang them from your ceiling at varying lengths. You can also weave some fairy lights through them to add a Christmassy glow.

You will need:

- Glue gun
- Glue sticks
- 9 paper party bags (per snowflake)
- Pencil
- Scissors
- Battery-operated LED fairy lights (optional)
- Cotton or string
- Pokey tool (optional)
- Glittered snowflakes or acrylic gems

TOP TIP Adding a sparkly centre to each of your snowflakes is a must!

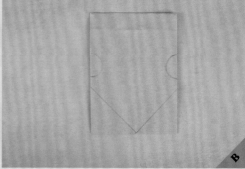

1 Plug in your glue gun to heat up.

2 Ensure that all of the bags are the same way round, with their openings facing away from you and their bases closest to you **(step A)**.

3 Sketch your design onto the open end of the top bag **(step B)**.

4 If you're feeling confident, you can start to cut out the design with some scissors straight away. I split up the bags into three sets of three and use the one with the original design as my template to cut around **(step C)**.

5 Using your glue gun, begin to glue your paper bags together. To do this, run a line of adhesive along the base of your first bag and a second line along the centre to create a T-shape **(step D)**.

6 Place a second bag on top, press firmly

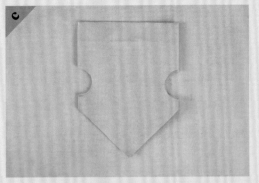

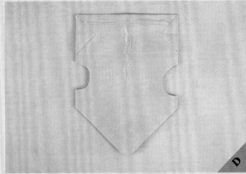

into place, then repeat the process with subsequent bags to create a stack **(step E)**.

7   Fan the bags out so that they form a circle, then glue the first and last bags together to create your snowflake shape. If using fairy lights, this is when you gently thread them through the holes in your design **(step F)**.

8   Thread a length of cotton or string through the top hole of your snowflake, or use your pokey tool to make a hole if necessary, and tie to create a loop.

9   Glue a pretty decoration to the centre of your snowflake to finish. This could be a glittered snowflake or an acrylic gem – your choice!

Christmas Tree Napkins

I always seem to feed the five thousand on Christmas Day, but I wouldn't have it any other way! These Christmas tree napkins are a must, especially if you're looking to add a touch of magic to your Christmas table without spending a ton of money.

After all, most of us have a set of fabric napkins that we pull out for the big day and this folding technique is so quick that, once you've mastered it, it's something you can do the night before.

These napkins look lovely on their own, but picking up some cinnamon sticks (which are really inexpensive) to tuck underneath as tree trunks will take your presentation to the next level.

You will need:

- Fabric napkins (I've used 20" x 20")
- Cinnamon sticks
- Ribbon or twine (optional)

TOP TIP If you want your folds to be completely smooth, iron your napkins first.

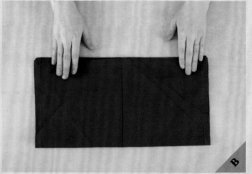

1. Smooth out your napkin on a hard, flat surface **(step A)**.

2. Fold the napkin in half lengthways **(step B)**.

3. Fold it in half again so that you are left with a square. Make sure the corners are completely lined up and there are no wrinkles in the fabric.

4. Turn your napkin towards you so that the four separate layers are directly in front of you **(step C overleaf)**.

5. Fold up the corner of each layer, one at a time, making sure to stagger them equally **(step D overleaf)**.

6. Slide one hand under the napkin and place the other on top, so that the fabric

is sandwiched between your hands. Flip it over **(steps E and F)**.

7   Fold both the left and right outer corners towards the centre. One should sit on top of the other **(steps G, H and I)**.

8   Flip the napkin over again **(step J)**.

9   Fold each of the corners up. After the first corner has been folded, tuck the remaining corners under the previous one **(step K)**.

10 Once all of the corners have been tucked under **(step L)**, pop a cinnamon stick underneath the napkin to give a tree-trunk effect. Tie a bow around the cinnamon with ribbon or twine for an extra wow factor.

Wood-slice Tree Decorations

I must admit to being one of those people who has multiple Christmas trees. While I love seeing the kids' lovely little decorations hanging on the tree, I also adore a really elegant, colour-coordinated affair. So, by having multiple trees, we get the best of both worlds! Having said that, these wood-slice decorations also give you the best of both worlds. They're a doddle to make with the kids and rustic enough to give your tree a really fresh and modern edge.

You will need:

- Drill and drill bit
- Wood slices
- Small paintbrush
- White acrylic paint
- Twine
- Black fine liner
- Acrylic paint markers in black, orange and red
- Glue gun
- Glue sticks
- Brown card

1   Drill a hole in the top of one of the wood slices **(step A)**.

2   For the snowman, take a paintbrush and cover the surface of the wood slice with white acrylic paint **(step B)**.

3   Set aside to dry for 30 minutes, then apply another coat if needed, leaving to dry for another 30 minutes.

4   Cut a length of twine and thread it through the hole in the top of the wood slice, then tie it in a knot to create a hanging **(step C)**.

5   Take a black fine liner or black acrylic paint marker and draw some eyes on the top third of the wood slice.

6 Take an orange acrylic paint marker and draw a carrot nose.

7 Use the black fine liner or acrylic paint marker to create a mouth on the bottom third **(step D)**.

8 Let the wood slice dry for 30 minutes.

9 For the reindeer, plug in your glue gun to heat up then repeat step 1 above.

10 Using a black fine liner or black acrylic marker draw a pair of eyes on the top third of the wood slice.

11 With a red acrylic marker, draw a nose in the centre of the piece and use a black pen draw a mouth under the red nose.

12 Create a pair of reindeer antlers out of brown card and use a dab of hot glue to adhere them to the back of the wood slice **(step E)**. So cute!

Christmas Fabric Baubles

How stylish are these fabric-covered baubles? You'd never know each one was just a bit of fabric over a polystyrene ball, would you? This project is an old favourite because it requires only a few bits and pieces but the finished result looks really expensive. What's more, you can use any fabric. They stand the test of time but, if you like, you can refresh them each year with different fabric to suit your tree's changing colour schemes.

You will need:

- Glue gun
- Glue sticks
- Square pieces of fabric, large enough to more than cover your bauble
- Spray adhesive for fabric
- Polystyrene balls or baubles
- Twine
- Thread
- Scissors
- Faux foliage or picks
- Ribbon

1   Plug in your glue gun to heat up.

2   Lay one of your fabric squares on a flat surface and spray it with a coating of adhesive.

3   Place your polystyrene ball in the centre of the fabric square **(step A)**.

4   Gather the sides of the fabric around the ball and use your hands to scrunch them together **(step B)**.

5   Tie a length of twine or thread around the scrunched-up fabric to secure it in place then use another length to create a hanging by looping it through the first piece and tying a knot.

6   Next, use a dab of glue to add a piece of faux foliage to the front of the bauble **(step C)**.

7   Cover the tied twine or thread with a length of ribbon then tie it into a bow **(step D)**.

8   Repeat steps 2–7 to make a set of baubles then hang them on your tree to make a fabulous festive statement!

Christmas Gonk

Gonks are still a huge trend in home décor – especially when it comes to the festive season – and their popularity doesn't look to be waning any time soon!

I think people's love of gonks comes from their playful and mischievous vibe while still looking stylish. If you haven't dabbled in the trend yet, this is the perfect project.

TOP TIP You can use any kind of pompom for this craft. The choice of coloured card and embellishments is also up to you, but here are some suggestions!

You will need:

- Glue gun
- Glue sticks
- Card
- Pencil
- Scissors
- Thread
- Furry or handmade pompom (see page 26 to make your own)
- Self-adhesive stars
- Small metal bell
- Small wooden bead or ball

1   Plug in the glue gun to heat up.

2   Draw a semi-circle onto some card with a pencil and then cut it out with a pair of scissors **(step A)**. The straight edge of the semi-circle needs to be the approximate circumference of the pompom.

3   Bring the two corners of the card around to create a cone shape, but don't glue them into place just yet.

4   Take a length of thread and fold it in half to create a loop for hanging. Use a dab of hot glue to secure the ends of the thread into place at the point of the cone **(step B)**.

5   Next, run a bead of glue along the length of card where the edges meet and press together to form your cone.

6   Run another bead of glue around the inside edge of the cone and press your pompom into place.

7   Set aside to dry for 30 minutes.

8   Next, decorate the gonk's hat with a couple of self-adhesive stars and use a dab of glue to add a bell to the top of the cone where the loop hanging is.

9   To give the gonk a nose, glue a small wooden ball or bead to where the hat and the pompom meet.

10 Hang your handmade festive gonk on your Christmas tree!

Faux Snow-globe Jars

For me, part of the fun of crafting and creating is sprucing up items that you already have in the home and giving them a new lease of life. For this project, you'll need some glass containers with suction lids. If you're anything like me, you'll probably have a fair few of them knocking around the kitchen! You'll be amazed by how great these snow globe-inspired jars look once you've given them a winter wonderland-style makeover.

TOP TIP You can use any figures that you like and feel free to tweak the colour scheme to suit your personal style.

You will need:

- Glue gun
- Glue sticks
- 3 different-sized glass jars with suction lids
- Miniature figures
- Miniature trees
- Faux snow
- Small paintbrush
- PVA glue
- Red liner tape
- 3 strings of battery-operated LED bottle lights
- Wood slice large enough to accommodate the jars
- Pine cones
- Faux Christmas picks
- Cinnamon sticks

1   Plug in the glue gun to heat up.

2   Use a dab of hot glue to adhere your miniature figures and trees to the base of each jar **(step A)**.

3   Sprinkle a small amount of faux snow over the base of each jar to hide any excess glue and give the effect of a carpet of snow **(step B)**.

4   Next, use a paintbrush to dab small dots of PVA glue to the insides of the jars. Then, sprinkle some more faux snow over the glue to give a snowy effect **(steps C and D)**.

5   Use strips of red liner tape to secure the battery packs of your bottle lights to the inside of each jar lid. Secure each lid in

place and allow the lights to hang freely inside the jars **(step E)**.

6 Set the jars aside for at least 30 minutes to dry completely.

7 Once the jars are dry, arrange them on the wood slice and add a few pine cones, faux picks and cinnamon sticks for decoration, either loose or glued into place as you wish.

8 Glue some additional faux picks to the tops of the jar lids to finish **(step F)**.

9 Your show-stopping festive centrepiece is now ready to impress your guests!

Cinnamon Stick Candle

If you're anything like me, you'll have some LED candles either on display in a room somewhere or stashed in a cupboard. They are so useful to have around the place.

You can quickly turn them from drab to fab ready for the Christmas season by simply adding a few cinnamon sticks, some ribbon and faux foliage. The delightful result will be a rustic centrepiece for your Christmas table or a cosy addition to your festive living room.

TOP TIP Create a couple of LED candles in different sizes for maximum impact.

You will need:

- Glue gun
- Glue sticks
- LED candle
- Long cinnamon sticks (at least two dozen)
- Scissors or sharp knife
- Hessian ribbon
- Gingham ribbon (or ribbon of your choice as long as its width does not exceed that of the hessian ribbon)
- Faux Christmas foliage or pick

1   Plug in your glue gun to heat up.

2   Take a look at how best to arrange your cinnamon sticks around your LED candle before gluing them in place. You may need to trim them with scissors or a sharp knife to suit your candle height. If your candle is of the type that is shorter at the front with more of an exposed flame, it's best to position longer sticks at the back of the candle and reserve shorter sticks for the front.

3   Start to adhere the cinnamon sticks to the surface of the LED candle, one by one, then leave the candle in an upright position to dry for 30 minutes **(steps A and B)**.

4   Cut a length of hessian ribbon long enough to wrap around the circumference of the candle and overlap slightly where the two ends meet. Glue into place **(step C)**.

5   Next, take your gingham ribbon, repeat step 4, then set your candle aside to dry for 30 minutes **(step D)**.

6   Once both ribbons have dried in place, glue your faux foliage or Christmas pick to the front centre of your candle **(step E)**.

7   Create a small bow from an offcut of gingham ribbon and glue into place over the foliage. Set aside to dry for 30 minutes.

No-sew Christmas Trees

Christmas is my absolute favourite time of year so it's no surprise that I'm always on the lookout for cute crafts that will add little festive touches to every room in my house.

I absolutely love it when something looks impressive and receives lots of lovely compliments – especially when you know that the piece was relatively easy to make (not that you need to tell anyone that!). That is exactly the case with these adorable no-sew Christmas trees!

You will need:

- Glue gun
- Glue sticks
- Drill and drill bit
- Wood slices
- Wooden dowels
- Scrap card or paper for a template
- Pencil
- Scissors
- Fat quarters of different fabrics
- Fabric adhesive
- Buttons
- Soft toy stuffing
- Twine
- Faux snow and finely shredded paper to decorate (optional)

1   Plug in your glue gun to heat up.

2   Take a wood slice and drill a hole in it's centre, snug enough for the dowel, so choose your drill bit accordingly. Place your dowel in the hole then use your glue gun to seal around its edge.

3   Using a pencil, sketch the outline of a Christmas tree onto some scrap card or paper. The tree needn't be a specific size but bear in mind that it should be roughly proportionate to your dowel and wood slice.

4   Cut your template with scissors. Use this to trace the shape onto two pieces of fabric then cut them out.

5   Once you have your two fabric shapes, choose the side of your fabric you want

as the outside of your tree. Glue around the inside edges of one piece with your glue gun or fabric adhesive, then stick the other piece on top, leaving space between the two pieces to fill with stuffing **(step A)**. You can also decorate the tree by adding small dots of glue down the centre line of the tree and adding some buttons. At this point, do not apply glue to the bottom 'tree trunk' edge so that you're able to add the stuffing. Set aside to dry for 30 minutes.

6   Start to add the stuffing to the inside of the tree. Use a pencil to help push the padding into the tight corners **(step B)**.

7   Tie a short length of twine into a bow around the dowel and carefully arrange some faux snow and finely shredded paper on the wood-slice base **(step C)**.

8   Take your wood-slice-and-dowel base and gently push the free end of the dowel into the stuffing via the 'tree trunk' opening. Then, carefully seal the opening with the glue gun or fabric adhesive. Make sure to add a little extra glue to secure the dowel in place. Set aside to dry for 30 minutes and you're done **(step D)**!

Yarn Christmas Trees

These yarn Christmas trees make a great addition to any stash of festive decorations. You can make a few of them in a variety of sizes and styles, but I think they look best in sets of three.

Once you've done the base layer of cream thread, for instance, you can really get creative with your choices of coloured yarn and the arrangement of the strands on top. The photographs here show a few different styles to inspire you but you could really go for any colour scheme that fits in with your personal festive look and feel!

You will need:

- Glue gun
- Glue sticks
- Card
- Pencil
- Scissors
- Yarn (I used a thicker cream yarn and a thin green)
- Gold string

TOP TIP   The yarn should feel secure but try not to overdo it with glue as you don't want to see large splodges of it on your tree!

1   Plug in your glue gun to heat up.

2   Draw a quarter-circle onto your card then cut it out with a pair of scissors. It really doesn't matter what size it is but it should have that all-important round edge **(step A)**.

3   Bring the two straight edges of the card together to form a cone shape. Glue them into place and set aside to dry for 30 minutes **(step B)**.

4   Add a small amount of glue to the tip of the cone and place the free end of yarn on top. Start to wind the yarn around the cone, using small dabs of glue to keep it in place as you go **(step C)**.

5   When the cone is completely covered in yarn, cut the thread at a suitable place and set the cone aside to dry for 30 minutes **(step D)**.

6   Once the glue is dry, you can start to layer the other colours of yarn and string onto the cone. Start with the green yarn – again, beginning at the top of the cone with a dab of glue then winding it loosely around the cone to give a draped effect. You'll only need a small amount of glue to keep these strands in place **(step E)**.

7   Repeat step 6 with the gold string **(step F)**.

8   Now you're ready to make your next tree!

Grapefruit Lip Balm

There's no better time to test out a new lip balm than winter, when our lips are most likely to be chapped and dry. And I don't know about you, but if I'm going to use a product on my body or face, I like to know exactly what's in it. So, if I can make it myself and be in control of those ingredients, then so much the better. This grapefruit version is especially moisturizing and smells amazing – give it a go!

You will need:

- 1½ tablespoons beeswax pellets
- 1½ tablespoons shea butter
- 1½ tablespoons coconut oil
- 50 drops or ½ teaspoon grapefruit essential oil (you can replace this with another essential oil if you like)
- Heatproof jug or bowl
- Spoon for mixing
- 5ml Travel-size cosmetic pots

For the decorative lids:
- Decorative papers
- Scissors
- PVA glue
- Small paintbrush

TOP TIP The beeswax pellets will take longer to melt than the other ingredients but they will get there – just keep on stirring!

1 Add the beeswax pellets, shea butter and coconut oil to a heatproof jug or bowl **(step A)**. Place the jug or bowl in the microwave and heat on a medium-high setting for 30 seconds. Stir the mixture, then heat again in 30-second bursts, checking and stirring after each interval until the ingredients have completely melted. Add the drops

of essential oil and stir to combine. Grapefruit oil doesn't have a particularly strong scent so you may need to use between 50 and 60 drops (½ teaspoon or so), depending on your personal preference.

2   With a steady hand, pour the mixture into the cosmetic pots. If you want to decorate the lids, set them to one side while you leave the mixture to solidify **(step B)**.

4   Use your lids as a template to create shapes of the same size on decorative paper. Cut out the shapes and adhere them to the lids with some PVA glue. I also like to add a stamped image as a second layer, which I fussy cut and glue in place **(steps C and D)**.

4   Screw the lids back on the pots, then leave everything in a cool space to solidify further for at least one hour (step E).

Once cooled, enjoy your gorgeous new lip balms, or give them as gifts to friends and family!

Gilding Flake Vase

Out of all the things I've made, this gold-and-black vase has to be one of my favourite pieces – a bold statement, I know! I've always been amazed by what you can make yourself at home and when I started experimenting with gilding flakes, which we often use in the craft industry for decoration, I knew I had to try them on a vase. I wasn't disappointed!

For anyone who hasn't used gilding flakes before, they're basically small metallic flakes that you can use to embellish paper, card, glass or myriad other surfaces. I'm sure that once you try them, you'll want to use them to bring some bling to all sorts of projects.

You will need:

- Protective gloves
- Clear glass vase
- Medium paintbrush
- Gilding flake glue
- Gilding flakes
- Masking tape
- Empty cardboard box
- Black spray paint

TOP TIP If you don't fancy getting too messy, wear a pair of protective gloves.

1   Pop on your protective gloves, if using. Use a paintbrush to daub some glue over the inside surface of the vase in sections **(step A)**.

2   Set the vase aside for a couple of minutes to allow the PVA glue to go slightly tacky.

3   Meanwhile, clean and dry your paintbrush, then dip it into the gilding flakes and apply them to the glued sections inside the vase **(step B)**.

4   Tape around the neck and rim of the vase, to prevent any paint from being sprayed on the outside of the glass during the next step **(step C)**.

5 Take the cardboard box, vase and black spray paint outside. Place the vase inside the box, then spray the inside of the glass vase until it is completely coated and opaque **(step D)**.

6 Leave the vase to dry for at least two hours, then give it another coat, if needed, and leave to dry. Once you're happy with the paint finish, remove the masking tape.

7 Finish off this luxurious-looking piece with an arrangement of your favourite faux flowers.

Sock Snowman

This is a fantastic project to do with the kids in the run-up to Christmas. They will have a ball filling up the socks with handfuls of rice and will delight in choosing their favourite-coloured socks for the hats and scarves.

TOP TIP To create a bunny version of this craft for Easter, simply divide the sock into two sections, as below, then secure an elastic tie around the top of the smaller section for the head and split the top section into two parts for the ears!

You will need:

- Scissors
- 1 white sock
- Uncooked rice
- Elastic bands
- 1 coloured or fluffy sock
- Black card
- Hole punch
- PVA glue
- Pipe cleaner
- Small acrylic gems or snowflakes

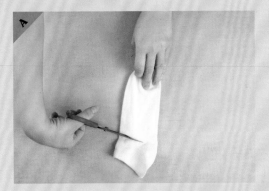

1 Take a pair of scissors and trim the white sock just above the heel **(step A)**.

2 Fill the sock with rice and tie off the top with an elastic band **(step B)**.

3 Take another elastic band and secure it in place approximately one-third of the way from the top to create a head and a body **(step C)**.

4 Take the coloured or fluffy sock and trim just above the heel, as you did with the first sock.

5 This time, use the top part of the sock to create the snowman's hat. Start by cutting the non-elasticated end into strips to create the tassel part of the hat **(step D)**.

6   Next, pop the elasticated opening of the sock onto the head of the snowman and secure an elastic tie around the tassels to fashion a hat shape **(step E)**.

7   Trim a strip of the leftover coloured sock to make the scarf then tie it around the snowman's neck.

8   Punch or cut eight holes into some black card. Use a dab of PVA glue to stick them onto the snowman's head to create two eyes and a smile.

9   Cut a small section of pipe cleaner for a carrot nose and glue it into place between the eyes and the smile.

10 Glue a couple of gems or snowflakes down the middle of the snowman's body for buttons **(step F)**.

11 Set aside to dry and hey presto – a squashy, friendly snowman for everyone to enjoy!

Bobble-hat Bunting

Would you believe me if I told you that all you need to make these cute little hats are some empty toilet-roll tubes and some yarn?

In my opinion, this bunting is the perfect last-minute Christmas decoration. What's more, you could use the bobble-hat technique for all sorts of things, such as cute gift-wrapping decorations or individual tree hangings.

You will need:

- 4 toilet-roll tubes
- 2 balls of yarn in your choice of colours
- Cotton wool for padding
- Scissors
- Small and medium wooden beads

1 Cut your toilet-roll tubes into strips measuring around an inch in width.

2 Create multiple 7.5" long strands from two different-coloured balls of yarn.

6 Once the cardboard strip is completely covered, push the loose strands of yarn back through the centre of the tube **(steps D and E)**.

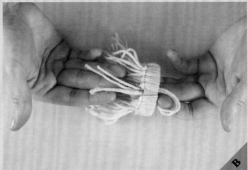

3 Take two strands at a time and fold them in half **(step A)**.

4 Pass them under one of the toilet-roll tube strips then thread the loose ends through the looped end. Pull the strands tight to make a knot **(step B)**.

5 Repeat until the toilet-roll tube is completely covered in looped yarn **(step C)**.

7   Use a small piece of cotton wool to pad out the inside of the hat **(step F)**.

8   Tie a length of yarn around the loose strands to create the bobble top **(step G)**.

9   Neaten any excess strands by trimming them to size.

10 Repeat steps 3–9 to create multiple bobble hats. Then, cut a long strand of yarn and begin to thread the bobble hats onto it, adding three wooden beads between every hat to space them evenly.

11 Drape or hang your bobble-hat bunting!

Cookie-jar Gift

This is a brilliant gift and something you can put together very easily with the kids. They'll feel as if they've really bought into the activity, and because the jar doesn't take too long to assemble, they won't get bored either.

This jar will make a great gift for a teacher or anyone with a birthday during the festive season. You can even switch out the paper used in the lid to suit the recipient.

TOP TIP Write the recipe method on any large gift tag you have to hand – or you can create your own!

You will need:

- A 34oz Mason jar
- Sheet of patterned paper
- Scissors
- Pencil
- Spoon
- 8oz self-raising flour
- 2oz cocoa powder
- 4 ½oz brown sugar
- 4 ½oz caster sugar
- 2 ½ox milk chocolate, broken into small chunks
- 2 ½ white chocolate, broken into small chunks
- Large gift tag (or some card to make your own)
- Twine

1   Clean the jar thoroughly in a dishwasher. Remove the waxed disc from inside.

2   Using the waxed disc as a template, draw a circle onto your patterned paper, then cut it out with your scissors **(step A)**.

3   Insert the paper circle into the lid between the ring part and the waxed seal. Set to one side **(step B)**.

4   Use a spoon to transfer the dry ingredients to the jar. Create a series of equal layers, starting with the self-raising flour.

5   Alternate the different layers until you have used up all the ingredients **(steps C and D)** and replace the lid.

6 Write the instructions below onto a large tag. (Alternatively, type them up, print them off and stick them to the tag!) Then, take a length of twine, thread it through the tag and tie it around the neck of the jar to create a rustic finish.

> Preheat the oven to 180°C. Add 4.5oz softened butter to a mixing bowl, add one egg and beat. Add the contents of the jar and mix well. Divide the dough into small, walnut-sized pieces and space them evenly on a baking tray lined with greaseproof paper. Bake in the oven for 8–10 minutes, leave to cool on a wire rack and enjoy!

7 Gift your jar to a deserving loved one or friend!

Christmas Treat Bauble

If you're searching for a great family craft project, look no further . . . And with tasty treats inside, these baubles are the gift that keeps on giving!

You can hang them on the tree as decorations containing a hidden surprise, or use them as an alternative to wrapping paper for smaller presents. They also make great end-of-term gifts for teachers.

TOP TIP Make sure your square of fabric is completely saturated with fabric stabilizer to give it the stiffness needed to retain its shape.

You will need:

- 12" x 12" fabric squares
- Scissors
- Balloons
- Scrap paper to protect your surfaces
- Fabric stabilizer
- Elastic bands
- Small treats
- Ribbon
- Thread

1   Fold your fabric square in half, from corner to corner, to create a triangle.

2   Next, fold in half a further three times, snip around the edge with your scissors and unfold to create a circle (step A).

3   Inflate a balloon to the approximate size you'd like your finished bauble to be (step B).

4   Put a piece of scrap paper under the fabric then spray with fabric stabilizer until it is thoroughly soaked (step C).

5   Place the balloon in the middle of your fabric circle and gather the sides of the fabric around it to create a round bauble shape.

6   Pinch the edges of the fabric together at the top and secure in place with an elastic band (step D).

7   Apply more fabric stabilizer to any dry patches around the top of your fabric bauble shape.

8   Leave to dry for 30 minutes.

9   Once the fabric is completely dry, snip the elastic band, gently open out the top of your bauble slightly and pierce the balloon inside.

10 Remove the deflated balloon and fill your fabric bauble with sweets or small treats **(step E)**.

11 Tie a length of ribbon around the top of your bauble to secure, then finish with a bow.

12 Pass a length of thread under the ribbon at the back of the bauble and tie it off to create a loop.

Lunar New Year Lanterns

I made these lovely lanterns a few years back, to decorate the house for Lunar New Year, and thought I'd give them a bit of an update. Not only do they look really impactful, they're a quick and easy way to decorate your home for New Year's Eve!

TOP TIP Paper lanterns are fantastic party decorations no matter the occasion. Simply switch out the paper to fit the celebration!

You will need:

- Two sheets of patterned paper
- Scissors or guillotine
- Red liner tape
- Craft mat or suitable cutting surface
- Ruler
- Pencil
- Craft knife or Stanley knife
- Hole punch or pokey tool
- Ball of twine

1   Cut a rectangle of patterned paper measuring 11" x 6".

2   Choose another piece of paper with a different print and cut a second rectangle measuring 12" x 5" **(step A)**.

3   Take the 12" x 5" piece and add a strip of red liner tape along the 12-inch sides and down one of the 5-inch sides **(step B)**.

4 Next, take the 11" x 6" piece of patterned paper and set it down on a craft mat or surface that you don't mind cutting into. Create a fold 1 inch down from the top and 1 inch up from the bottom **(step C)**.

5 Using a Stanley knife or craft knife (and pressing very lightly), cut strips measuring 1 inch in width between the two folds. Continue to cut these strips across until you have eleven equal-sized strips in total.

6 Fold the top 1-inch width sections at the top and bottom of the piece of paper inwards **(step D)**.

7 Remove the backing from all the strips of red liner tape on the 12" x 5" piece of paper and set it down, tape-side up **(step E)**.

8 Next, take the 11" x 6" piece of paper and lay this on top of the first piece. Use the top and bottom tabs that you created in step 6 to adhere the pieces to one another and press into place **(step F)**.

9 Once the two pieces are joined together, bring the shorter edges of the piece around so that the two meet to produce a lantern shape and press into place **(step G)**.

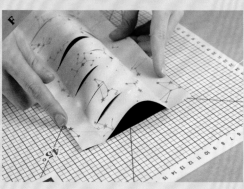

11 Use a hole punch or pokey tool to create a hole in either side of each lantern.

12 Take your ball of twine and thread the free end through the holes in the lanterns. Once you've finished, cut the twine to the length you require for your garland.

10 Repeat steps 1–9 until you have the desired number of lanterns for your garland.

13 Hang the garland from your ceiling or across your window to create the ultimate party backdrop!

Acknowledgements

First of all, I want to say that writing this book has been a dream come true. I've been in this industry for many years but I'm still so passionate about what I do, and there's nothing I love more than people discovering crafting and creating for the first time. For me, this book is very much a love letter to the members of our wonderful craft community who enable me to continue to live out this dream every day!

A huge thank-you to my family for their unwavering support in everything I want to achieve. To my mam, dad, Helen, Matt, Val, John, Simon and my boys – none of this would be possible without you.

Thank you to my Crafter's Companion team, who go above and beyond every day. And a huge thank-you to Bianca, Ash and Jodie, who helped me to pull together all of the wonderful projects and imagery.

To my publisher, Susanna Wadeson, and the amazing team at Transworld, especially Steph Duncan, Phil Evans, Rebecca Wright, Beci Kelly, Tony Maddock, Becky Short, Melissa Kelly, everyone in Sales and Bobby Birchall at Bobby & Co – thank you.
I am beyond grateful to you for bringing this book to life!

Thank you to my agents, Paul Stevens and Laura Hill, and the team at Independent Talent.

Finally, thank you for reading this book. Whether you're new to crafting or have been doing it for years, I hope *Craft Your Year* has been a friendly guide and has inspired you to take some time for yourself to get creative.

About the Author

Sara Davies MBE is the youngest-ever female investor to appear on BBC One's Dragons' Den and is well known as the founder and creative director of the global craft business, Crafter's Companion. Launched while she was still at university, Crafter's Companion is now a global business selling papercraft, art, needlecraft and stationary items across 40 countries, with head offices in the US and UK. Sara lives with her husband and sons in Teesside.

To find out more about Sara, read her bestselling auto-biography *We Can All Make It: The Secrets of Success, My Story.*

Craft Index

A

Air Freshener, DIY 98
Autumnal Wreath 110

B

Bag, Gift 30
Bag, Witch's Broom Treat 116
Bath Salts Jar 42
Bauble, Christmas Treat 184
Bauble, Glass Terrarium 102
Baubles, Christmas Fabric 162
Baubles, Decorated Ceramic 146
Bird Feeder 132
Bobble-hat Bunting 180

C

Candle, Cinnamon Stick 168
Candle, Citronella 138
Candle, LED Découpage 80
Candle Holder, LED, Doily 62
Candle Holder, Wooden Ball 128
Candy-cane Santa Place
    Settings 150
Canvas, Glue Gun 130
Card, Father's Day Shaker 100
Card, Mother's Day 40
Christmas Fabric Baubles 162
Christmas Garland or Wreath 144
Christmas Gonk 164
Christmas Treat Bauble 184
Christmas Tree Napkins 156
Christmas Trees, No-sew 170
Christmas Trees, Yarn 172
Cinnamon Stick Candle 168
Citronella Candle 138
Clay Trinket Tray 120
Cookie-jar Gift 182

D

Decorated Ceramic Baubles 146
Decorations, Wood Tree Slice 160
DIY Air Freshener 98
Doily LED Candle Holder 62
Dried Flower Hanging 126

E

Easter Bunny Wreath 50
Easter Treat Jars 48

F

Father's Day Gift 82
Father's Day Shaker Card 100
Faux Snow-globe Jars 166

Floating Ghosts 112
Floral Macramé Wreath 68
Flower Heart Frame 44
Flower Napkin Rings 88
Flower, Dried Hanging 126
Flower, Pressed, Frame 104
Foot Scrub 22

G

Garland, Christmas 144
Ghosts, Floating 112
Gift Bag 30
Gift box, Valentine's Day 34
Gift, Cookie-jar 182
Gift, Father's Day 82
Gilded Wall Sconce 90
Gilding Flake Vase 176
Glass Bauble Terrarium 102
Glossary 14
Glue Gun Canvas 130
Gonk, Christmas 164
Gonk, Plant Pot 118
Grapefruit Lip Balm 174

H

Hairband 96
Hessian Pumpkins 114

L

LED Découpage Candle 80
Lemon Coasters 92
Lip Balm, Grapefruit 174
Lunar New Year Lanterns 186

M

Macramé Coasters 122
Macramé Feathers 134
Macramé Plant Hanger 54
Macramé, Floral Wreath 68
Marbled Mug 72
Mother's Day Card 40

N

No-sew Christmas Bag 148
No-sew Christmas Trees 170
No-sew Cushion Cover 60

O

Orange Drinks Tray 76
Organizer 18
Origami Flowers 56

P

Painted Rock Photo Holder 74
Paper Bag Snowflakes 154

Photo, Painted Rock Holder 74
Photo, Valentine's Wooden
    Cube 38
Plant Pot Gonk 118
Pompom Easter Bunny Pots 50
Pompom Making 26
Pompom Mirror 86
Pressed Flower Frame 104
Pumpkins, Hessian 114
Pumpkins, Sock 108

R

Ribbon Flowers 78
Rope Basket 140
Rope Tray 124
Rose and Aloe Vera Clay Face
    Mask 20

S

Shower Steamers 84
Snow-effect Jars 152
Snowflakes, Paper Bags 154
Snow-globe, Faux, Jars 166
Sock Pumpkins 108
Sock Snowman 178
Spring Wreath 24
Succulent Plant Pots 94

T

Toolkit 12

V

Valentine's Day Gift Box 34
Valentine's Wooden Photo
    Cube 38

W

Water Effect Flower Vase 66
Witch's Broom Treat Bag 116
Wooden Ball Candle Holder 128
Wood-slice Tree Decorations 158
Wreath, Autumnal 110
Wreath, Christmas 144
Wreath, Easter Bunny 50
Wreath, Floral Macramé 68
Wreath, Spring 24

Y

Yarn Christmas Trees 172